What others
*True Love Begins With God*

"When I was young, there was a popular song that declared, love is a many splendored thing. We think of the many splendors of God's love for us. Pastor Bob has sought to point out and describe to us the many beautiful facets of God's love for us in his new book, True Love Begins With God. We encourage you to experience the riches of God's love for you as you read and discover for yourself, that true love, indeed begins with God."
Pastor Chuck Smith
Calvary Chapel of Costa Mesa, California

"In this remarkable study on the Love of God, Pastor Bob Claycamp draws one into the loving arms of Christ as he artfully explores the essential truths and power of God's transforming and life changing love in the life of a believer. This book provides practical, real-life guidance for those seeking renewal in their relationships through a deeper understanding of God's love."
Marian C. Eberly, LCSW, RN., BCPCC, PhD/c
Author, Conference Speaker and Christian Counselor

"How true the title of Bob Claycamp's book is: True Love Begins With God. Were it not for God, whose very nature is love, man wouldn't have a clue as to what true love really is. As Bob takes a 'fresh look at 1 Corinthians 13,' we get practical insights into these dynamic verses, insights that are inspiring, encouraging and challenging as to how true love translates into an everyday relationship with one's spouse. This book will be used over and over again as a long-awaited for and much needed tool by every pastor, as we have the opportunity to encourage those in our fellowships in the way of true love."
Richie Furay
Rock & Roll Hall of Fame, 1997, Buffalo Springfield
Pastor of Calvary Chapel of Broomfield, Colorado

# TRUE LOVE BEGINS WITH GOD

BY

## BOB CLAYCAMP

**Published by**

WORD PRODUCTIONS

www.wordproductions.org

*True Love Begins with God*
by Bob Claycamp

Published by Word Productions LLC

Copyright © 2011 by Bob Claycamp
Printed in the United States of America
ISBN 978-0-9909245-1-7

All Scripture quotations, unless otherwise indicated, are taken from the *The Holy Bible*, New King James Version © 1984 by Thomas Nelson, Inc.

**Robert D. Claycamp**
14201 N. 32nd Street
Phoenix, Arizona 85032
www.bobclaycamp.com

*To Jeanne, my precious wife,*

*the love of my youth*

*and love of my old age.*

*You're my closest friend,*

*confidant, and unconditional lover.*

# TABLE OF CONTENTS

# ACKNOWLEDGEMENTS

Jeanne—you've stood by me in so many of my wild ideas and dreams. You've faithfully prayed me through each and every one of them. I love you.

Micah, Jesse, and Chris—you're a picture of God's grace to me as I think of all that we've been through as a family. Carry on the heritage.

The elders of Calvary Chapel North Phoenix—thanks for your unending support of my calling, my 'experiments,' and my leadership.

Those that edited my manuscript—Pastor Chris and Gwen, Pastor Rudy, Leta, Maureen, Dave, Cheryline, Pam, Dolly, Michelle. Without your help this book wouldn't have happened.

Micah and Floyd—great work on the cover of this book.

The congregation of Calvary Chapel North Phoenix—you're the best congregation in the whole world. Thank you for your prayers and faithfulness.

The Lord Jesus—thank You for calling me to Yourself, loving me unconditionally, and bearing my sin. You're my best friend. I'm eternally grateful to You!

# 1 CORINTHIANS 13

*1 Though I speak with the tongues of men and of angels, but have not love, I have become sounding brass or a clanging cymbal.*

*2 And though I have the gift of prophecy, and understand all mysteries and all knowledge, and though I have all faith, so that I could remove mountains, but have not love, I am nothing.*

*3 And though I bestow all my goods to feed the poor, and though I give my body to be burned, but have not love, it profits me nothing.*

*4 Love suffers long and is kind; love does not envy; love does not parade itself, is not puffed up;*

*5 does not behave rudely, does not seek its own, is not provoked, thinks no evil;*

*6 does not rejoice in iniquity, but rejoices in the truth;*

*7 bears all things, believes all things, hopes all things, endures all things.*

*8 Love never fails. But whether there are prophecies, they will fail; whether there are tongues, they will cease; whether there is knowledge, it will vanish away.*

*9 For we know in part and we prophesy in part.*

*10 But when that which is perfect has come, then that which is in part will be done away.*

*11 When I was a child, I spoke as a child, I understood as a child, I thought as a child; but when I became a man, I put away childish things.*

*12 For now we see in a mirror, dimly, but then face to face. Now I know in part, but then I shall know just as I also am known.*

*13 And now abide faith, hope, love, these three; but the greatest of these is love.*

# INTRODUCTION

It seems that everyone is looking to find their true love. Much of this is fashioned by movies, music, and mystery. Just when we think we've found the love of our life, the unfortunate happens: they sin against us. Sure, we're not so perfect either. But still we're left crushed and angry. We can't believe that it happened to us.

So we cut our losses and head out once again to find that special someone. But how many someones are we suppose to go through before we find our perfect soulmate? And what about all the heartache, disappointment, and disillusionment that occurs in the mean time?

There's good news in the middle of all this. True love can be found. But we have to look in the right place. There IS a manual to find true love. It's called the Holy Bible. In its pages we find the road map to discovering our true love.

I believe the Bible tells us true love begins with God Himself. He created us. He fashioned us in His own image. He knows what we need, what we want, and what we think we must have. He's the foundation for that true love. God is love. Why then should we think He doesn't understand or care about our longing for love?

The greatest display of God's love was when He sent His only begotten Son into the world. Whoever would believe on Him would not perish but have everlasting life (John 3:16). We also find that God has given us a description of His love in some detail. It's found in what I believe is one of the most important chapters of the entire Bible: 1 Corinthians 13.

There we read how the Holy Spirit impressed upon the heart and mind of the apostle Paul what the believers in the city of Corinth needed so desperately. This is also what we need so desperately today. God's love is more important than all of our knowledge, our spiritual gifts, and our connections to important people. God's love not only changes us in this life, it lasts throughout eternity.

But what does this love of God look like? How will it show itself as it's lived out in our personal lives, marriages, and families? That's what this book is all about.

There are sixteen attributes of God's love detailed by the apostle Paul in 1 Corinthians 13:4-8. Seven of them are put in the positive (what God's love is like), and nine of them are described in the negative (what God's love does NOT look like).

The absolutely wonderful thing about God's love is that He puts His love into every person who places trust in His Son, Jesus Christ, for their salvation. We don't have to work up a holy love for others. We've been given His love as a gift. He's called us to simply pour out His love into every arena of life.

You'll find that I've shared with you a few aspects of my own personal life at the beginning of each chapter. Those anecdotes were selected to help give a practical illustration of that chapter's attribute of God's love. Then we'll examine that particular attribute of God's love, followed by a few considerations of what that aspect looks like in daily life.

At the end of the book, I've included a discussion guide. There are five questions that relate to the subject of each chapter. The guide can be used as a tool for small group settings or to deepen your own devotional times. May the God of love and comfort use this book to bring you into an overflowing experience of His love.

# CHAPTER 1

## ～✑ OUR TRUE SOULMATE ✑✑

In the spring of 1968, while I was having lunch with some friends in our high school cafeteria, up walked this gorgeous young thing. She asked about my friend, Steve, who was the drummer of our rock band. I knew Steve had another girlfriend, so I introduced myself as the bass player of the band. To my surprise she actually spent some time talking to me!

Our rock band, the Music Box, was a participant in a televised battle of the bands on the local CBS affiliate in Portland, Oregon. The winner was given an audition at Capitol Records in Hollywood, California.

Since this young lady, Jeanne Wyatt, seemed to be wowed by the mystique of our band, I decided to take the risk: I asked her to go with me to the television station and sit in on the taping of our session. She agreed. That began a hot and heavy relationship that lasted all through the next year and a half of high school.

After graduation, we eventually surrendered our lives to Christ. In a few weeks I resigned from the band. Jeanne and I married six months after our high school graduation. We were eighteen years old. We were each other's soulmate. We thought there was nothing that could get in the way of our love. We had the Lord. We had each other. We had everything we needed... until we started selfishly offending one another.

Walls began to build up between us. The glow and hope of youthful dreams were crashing down all around us. Even though we were Christians, we'd lost perspective of what true love was all about.

Our band, the Music Box, 1968 - 1969

Our wedding day, January 1, 1970

Through the brokenness of our hearts we came back to that individual foundation of God's love through Christ. We asked each other's forgiveness and through the wise counsel of other more mature believers, and the power of the Holy Spirit of God, we rebuilt our relationship step by step. Today, after over forty years of marriage, we're more in love than ever before. But we've had to humble ourselves before God and one another over the years. We've had to continually draw from the well of God's love as the love foundation of our lives.

## A GOD-BASED LOVE

It seems that although we think we understand true love, most of what we fall back on is a human-based love instead of a God-based love. The problems start when we try to fulfill certain unrealistic expectations we picked up long ago.

We can hop from relationship to relationship because we're addicted to that first little high school spark of puppy love. Anything short of that isn't real for us. But with that mind set, we rob ourselves of what God intended; and we live a very hurtful life, experiencing a lot of soul damage.

It's important to understand that true love begins with God. A lot of us can't even recognize true love. Instead, what we're involved in is selfish desire. That's what God wants to have changed in us, creating something entirely new and different.

So much of human-based love is founded upon selfish desires. We want to feel accepted, we want to have our deepest needs met, we want someone to make us feel that we're the most important thing on earth. But the common denominator is *me*. It's all about me; and that's not what true love is all about.

Men and women are desperately looking for their long lost soulmate. It seems to be the main goal, to find that special someone who will be the one who finally makes life complete. How is this term soulmate defined? You'll find various and sundry attempts at this by a website search engine. Some have defined it as one who naturally shares your deep feelings and attitudes. Others have said that it's your perfect person, the one you look for sometimes forever that completes you, that makes you feel like nothing can go wrong when they're near and they're always there for you. But how many partners must one go through before finding that one who fits the definition of the perfect soulmate?

Is there a manual for true love? One would think that after so many years of publishing books on love, someone would get it right. But the search goes on and sadness creeps into the human heart. How people yearn to find true love!

## IN THE BEGINNING...

I want to tell you some great news. There IS a manual to help you discover your true love. It's free, you don't have to be a member, you don't have to sign up for anything, and you don't have to give them your credit card number. It's called the Holy Bible.

It's true that God has revealed His general attributes through His creation. But He has more clearly revealed Himself through His Word. The Bible is God's word. It reveals to us that God is love. God doesn't try to love, He is love. It's His nature, and He is love in its purest form and in its highest sense.

The Bible tells us that God created man and woman to be relational creatures. It's part of our being created in the image of God. It's not instinct; we're not mere animals although we can behave like them at times. Having this relational desire is an integral feature of our soul.

Think about this: the very first soulmate for Adam was not Eve; it was God. On the sixth day of creation God created Adam. They immediately had fellowship with one another. Eve hadn't been created yet.

God gave Adam the responsibility to name the animals He had already created. There was something that He wanted Adam to see and understand. Adam watched the animals come two by two as he named them. But he began to perceive that for him, there wasn't a helper comparable to him.

What does the term a helper comparable mean? Its core meaning is: to surround, to protect, to come to the aid of, to help. Eve was to be the one to bring something into Adam's life that God saw Adam so desperately needed. God Himself stated that it wasn't good that the man should be alone.

Once God brought the woman to the man at the end of the sixth day, it says at the end of Genesis 1, "God saw everything that He had made, and indeed it was very good."

It was very good until Adam and Eve sinned against God. The relationship between him and her was immediately affected. Instead of the closeness, the complete openness, the vulnerability, and the security they once had, their sin brought a division between them.

There was this sense of shame each one felt. It led to attempts to cover themselves using dead fig leaves, which indirectly represented the fact that they were using their own efforts to cover their sin and shame.

When we sin against one another, it doesn't draw us closer together. When we as a husband or as a wife sin against our spouse, it makes us feel distanced from the other. We even stop communicating with each other because of the offenses that have built up. We refuse to speak for hours, even days and there's no forgiveness.

It's no longer about the issue that caused the argument. Now it's the principle of the thing. "I'm not going to be the first one to talk because they offended me," we say. "And if they don't say I'm sorry, I'm certainly not going to." It turns into a real battle. The reality is that we're not walking in the love of God. The longer we remain in that state, the more it gives the devil a foothold to destroy our relationship. That's his goal: to steal, to kill, and to destroy. If he can crush the affection in our hearts toward our spouses, children, or other people, he's accomplished his desire.

## THE FIRST MENTION OF LOVE

What does the Bible say about love? Did you know that love is talked about over 400 times in the Bible?

One of the principles of good biblical interpretation is called the principle of first mention. The principle of first mention is this: when an important word or concept occurs for the first time in the Bible, the context in which it occurs sets the pattern for its primary usage and development all through the rest of Scripture.

Let's apply this to the concept of love. We might think we should find the first mention of love in Genesis 1, 2 or even 3. But we don't find the word 'love' until we get to Genesis 22.

**Genesis 22:1-2**
*¹Now it came to pass after these things that God tested Abraham, and said to him, "Abraham!" And he said, "Here I am." ² Then He said, "Take now your son, your only son Isaac, whom you love, and go to the land of Moriah, and offer him there as a burnt offering on one of the mountains of which I shall tell you."*

Since the Holy Spirit was moving upon holy men of God to record the things in the Scripture, why does the word love first occur here in the Bible? I believe it's because of the context. It is found in the account of the love of a father toward his only son. God wanted us to understand that the truest expression of real love isn't the love of a man to a woman or a woman to a man. He wanted us to see that the highest example of love was the love of a father to his only son.

Our heavenly Father's love toward His only begotten Son, Jesus the Messiah, is what this points to. It's interesting that the first mention of love in the New Testament is found in Matthew 3:17, which says, *This is My beloved Son, in whom I am well pleased.* The first mention of love in John's gospel is none other than John 3:16: *For God so loved the world that He gave His only begotten Son, that whoever believes in Him should not perish, but have everlasting life.*

I personally believe that the starting place to find true love is found in the person of God Himself. He should be our true, foundational soulmate.

Now, I'm not saying that the love between a man and woman is insignificant; but there's a reason why God placed love in the context of Genesis 22 first in the Scriptures. It has to do with where we'll find true love as our foundation. Without the basis of His love in our lives, we'll naturally try to draw from others' love. When they fail us it's one more disappointment after another.

God's love for us is unconditional and pure. It has our best interest at its core. It's a healing love that's refreshing and exactly what we need. God has opened the door for us to have a restored relationship with Him, which leads us to experience the kind of fellowship and intimate sharing with Him.

Humans have the capacity to love because it's a God-given attribute; the problem is that sin has saturated the nature of man, and that sin even corrupts human love. That's why there's such a desperate need for all people to draw from a fountain of love that's outside of the human source. Man's love is corrupt because of sin and that sin initiates all manner of selfish desires. Then, those selfish desires are revealed through efforts of self-fulfillment, self-gratification, self-expression, self-exaltation, and self-focus. It's all about self.

This results in a corrupted love, a damaged soul, and a broken heart of disillusionment. The question then becomes, "Where else can I find it?" But true love begins with God, not man.

When we surrender to the love of God, something changes on the inside. The Holy Spirit moves in and makes His home in our lives. God's love is the primary expression of the Holy Spirit in our lives. The fruit of the spirit is love, and that love is expressed by joy, peace, and longsuffering.

## PERFORMANCE-BASED LOVE

Let's take a look again at 1 Corinthians 13 and think through the first three verses.

**1 Corinthians 13:1-3**
*[1]Though I speak with the tongues of men and of angels, but have not love, I have become sounding brass or a clanging cymbal. [2] And though I have the gift of prophecy, and understand all mysteries and all knowledge, and though I have all faith, so that I could remove mountains, but have not love, I am nothing. [3] And though I bestow all my goods to feed the poor, and though I give my body to be burned, but have not love, it profits me nothing.*

What the apostle Paul mentions here are good works that help people. However, without God's love as the basis, we're told they're profitless. God's love is greater than even our best good works. I like how the Amplified Bible translates this section of 1 Corinthians 13:

> *¹ If I [can] speak in the tongues of men and [even] of angels, but have not love (that reasoning, intentional, spiritual devotion such as is inspired by God's love for and in us), I am only a noisy gong or a clanging cymbal.*

In other words, without God's love at the center, I'm just a noise maker without meaning.

> *² And if I have prophetic powers (the gift of interpreting the divine will and purpose), and understand all the secret truths {and} mysteries and possess all knowledge, and if I have [sufficient] faith so that I can remove mountains, but have not love (God's love in me) I am nothing (a useless nobody).*

We hear of Christian leaders and pastors who have outwardly done very great things. But then it's discovered that inwardly their life is full of sin, and they damage the faith of so many of the people in their churches.

> *³ Even if I dole out all that I have [to the poor in providing] food, and if I surrender my body to be burned {in order that I may glory}, but have not love (God's love in me), I gain nothing.*

You see, we're so oriented to perform to get acceptance. If we perform well on our job we get our bonuses. It's cause and effect. We so easily carry that over to God and think, "Okay God; watch me dance. Don't You love me now? Don't You love me more? Do You love me less when I can't dance? Actually, I'm not performing very well this month, God. And I've got these health issues that drain my energy. As a matter of fact, I've got these attitude issues, and I'm not behaving very well today. I need to really clean up my act so You'll love me and bless me."

The whole thought process is based upon performance. But God's love is not, and never has been, based upon our performance. We need to stop relying upon our works to get God to like us. We have to receive this truth by faith because we may not feel it at the moment; but it's what the Bible tells us is true.

When we yield to God's love, something will start happening inside of us. A new motivation will start taking place which was never there before. It'll cause us to want to do what is loving and right because that's the affect of God's love working within us.

Sometimes we even put pressure on those we love. We have these unspoken expectations they should meet, especially in those that involve us. We may not even see they are there, hiding behind rationalizations we've built up for years.

For those of us who are married, let's ask the Lord to show us if we're putting undue pressure on our spouses to perform in some way in areas we should be getting only from God.

For those of us who have children, let's make the same request of the Lord regarding them. When there's conflict in the home, and mom and dad are arguing and complaining against each other, it affects the children. They may not even know the details of what's behind the conflict, but because their whole world is insecure it affects their behavior.

Let's ask the Lord this question: "Lord, are we putting pressure on our children to perform to gain our acceptance? Should we be approaching the situation in an entirely different way?" Let's ask the same question concerning the people we work with and say, "God, what would it look like in our daily work involvements to be saturated with Your love?"

When we plant a seed in fertile soil, the fruit which that plant will bear will be of the highest quality. The same is true with us as believers in Christ. When we're rooted and grounded in the seed bed of God's love, natural expressions of His love will show through in our life.

God wants us to know experientially what His love is like. Maybe we've been looking for love in all the wrong places. We need to get back to the source of true love. It begins with God, not man.

Actually, it begins with the God-man, Jesus Christ. He loves us so much that He came to this earth, bore our sins on the cross, and experienced death to pay for our sins.

He rose from the dead to show that the Father accepted what He did for us. Now the Father's offer is complete forgiveness. He says to us, "Your debt has been paid by My Son. Put your trust in Him, and join My family; all your sins are forgiven, past, present, and future."

True love begins with God. Let's stop trying to get that true love from others. Let's stop the expectations upon others that only God can fill. Let's allow our true soulmate to be the One and only God who created us.

# CHAPTER 2

## SATURATED WITH HIS LOVE

Many years ago, a friend of mine decided to go on a carrot juice diet. He purchased this very expensive juicer and a gunnysack full of carrots. He was so excited about the benefits to be experienced that he went overboard with the whole project. After a few days I noticed his skin was actually turning orange. My friend had been so saturated with carotene that it showed up on the surface of his body.

In the same way when God's love saturates our hearts, I believe it will show itself outwardly. We want everything God has available for us. Sometimes we have an idea of what that is. Maybe we want to have more faith. Possibly we want to have more courage. We want to see God heal our family, we want to see God heal our marriage, or we want everything to work out.

But what does God want? He's the One who purchased us. He initiated the whole process of drawing us to Himself. So the question we should be asking is this: "Lord, what do You want for me? What's important to You? I only want what You want for me. I'll set aside my laundry list of wants because I believe Your goodness surpasses my ability to understand my need." That's a pleasing thing to the Lord.

## THE DESIRE OF GOD FOR US

One of the most important things on the heart of God for us is that we would be saturated with His love. He desires that we would not only understand His love, but that our love would be impacted by His love so it affects how we live.

Jesus said, "By this all will know that you are My disciples, if you have love for one to another" (John 13:35). The love He was speaking of is defined by the Greek word *agape*'

This describes an unconditional love, a pure love, a love that originates from heaven, a love that shows itself in action and not merely with words. It's a love that's fully expressed by what God did in sending His Son to pay the ultimate sacrifice of death on the cross so that we can be reconciled to God and receive His forgiveness.

God's love is more valuable for us than all we can do for Him or than all the ways we can be used by Him. He wants us to be a distributor of His love, not merely a container of His love.

We need to have an outflow, like the Sea of Galilee, not merely an inflow with no outflow like the Dead Sea. God's desire is that our lives be saturated with His love because His love completely changes us.

Jesus said the two greatest commandments are to love God with all our heart, mind, soul, and strength; and to love our neighbor as ourselves. Let's examine those two commandments.

Take the first one; love God with all our heart, our mind, our soul, and our strength. Okay, do that. Notice the word all—every area of your heart, your mind, your soul, and your strength. If you do that, you have nothing left. You're wrung out like a dish rag.

Then He says, "Now love your neighbor as yourself." It's then that you have to say to God, "I've nothing left. I gave You everything; and now You're telling me to love my neighbor?"

I believe the key is this: we come to God empty so that He can fill us. This enables us to love our neighbor. But we first need to love the Lord, to trust Him—to trust Him so much that we release all concerns for ourselves. He's going to take care of us so we can be free to minister to others.

## WRAPPED UP WITH OURSELVES

Typically, what blocks loving others is that we're all wrapped up with ourselves. We're concerned God isn't going to come through for us.

Self-love is foundational to our nature because we think about ourselves more than we think about anything or anyone else. Think about your day yesterday. You were working, you were considering; but you were the center of the whole day.

Sometimes our self-love can even take on a negative, destructive expression. In this arena we still think about ourselves more often than we think about others; but our thoughts toward ourselves are thoughts of worthlessness, uselessness, self-pity, and self-loathing. This may have been conditioned by past abuse and the sins of others against us. The reality is, though, we're still thinking about ourselves, except this time it's in a negative way.

What God wants us to do as His children is to apply the truth from the Word of God about who we are in Him. Then we're to let this truth flush out all the other things that have been programmed into our lives as we've grown up.

Sometimes, because of the abuse and sins of others against us, we've been locked away and made unwilling to open up. It's too risky, too vulnerable.

God's love is a healing agent. To let God's love touch the deepest part of our souls is medicinal, it's healing, and it's refreshing. But it's also very scary because we're opening up doors to God that have been shut, locked, dead-bolted, chained, and barred because of the past hurt.

God created that deepest part of our lives, that area of our souls where the will, intellect, and feelings reside. He knows the damage that's there. He wants to heal us, but He wants His love to be what comes in and does the healing. God wants to flush out all those lying thoughts, but we've got to apply the Word of God and the shield of faith.

We need to ask Him to bring us to the point of such security in Him that we stop thinking so much about ourselves and focus on loving others. When we become convinced through the Word of God that God's love is so abundant, so filling, so healing, and so satisfying, it releases us to be conduits of His love, not merely containers.

## LOVE THAT SURPASSES OUR BAD BEHAVIOR

God wants to teach us how to love others, even those who become our enemies. That's how it was with us and God before we knew Him. We were enemies of God; and yet, He loved us while we were in sin.

God can be displeased with our behavior and attitudes and yet still love us, just like we can do with our own children and grandchildren. On the other hand, God can be pleased. It doesn't make Him love us more, but we can please the Lord when we walk according to His commandments.

It's a fascinating relationship aspect to think that we can please the Lord. He can't love us anymore than He already does even when we're having a bad day. But we can displease the Lord by allowing things into our lives that grieve His heart.

God desires that we be controlled by His Holy Spirit. Every attribute of His—the fact that He's immutable, the fact that He's eternal, the fact that He's infinite—all of those natural attributes are conditioned by the truth that He's a God of love. This is also true of His moral attributes—His kindness, mercifulness and His graciousness—all of those are conditioned by God's love.

Our spirit is that part of us which makes up the totality of who we are. If I take my spirit and impart it to my son, then he'll know experientially who I am, even though he may not follow that witness in his own life. This is what God has done with us when we've chosen to have faith in His Son, Jesus. God has sent His Spirit into our hearts that we might freely know Him. His Spirit is called the Holy Spirit because God is holy—not just love.

In 1 Corinthians 2:11-12, the Amplified Version puts it this way: *¹¹For what person perceives (knows and understands) what passes through a man's thoughts except the man's own spirit within him? Just so no one discerns (comes to know and comprehend) the thoughts of God except the Spirit of God. ¹² Now we have not received the spirit [that belongs to] the world, but the [Holy] Spirit Who is from God, [given to us] that we might realize {and} comprehend {and} appreciate the gifts [of divine favor and blessing so freely and lavishly] bestowed on us by God.*

For us to get to know God, He has to do something within us. He imparts to us His very Spirit that we might get to know Him. He wants us to know what He's like, to know His heart.

### Galatians 5:22-23
*²²But the fruit of the Spirit is love, joy, peace, longsuffering, kindness, goodness, faithfulness, ²³gentleness, self-control. Against such there is no law.*

When God's love reigns in the heart, joy will be a byproduct, peace will be a byproduct, longsuffering (which has to do with patiently enduring under difficult circumstances and having a positive outlook) will be a byproduct.

These expressions of God's love are what we find in 1 Corinthians 13. When we become a follower of the Lord Jesus, when we trust Christ for our salvation, God sends His Spirit into our heart, the center of our being. A relationship begins right then between us and Him when that indwelling takes place by the Holy Spirit.

The Holy Spirit is the earnest deposit of the full inheritance which will be given to us when we see Jesus face to face. The indwelling presence of the Holy Spirit is our mark of ownership. He owns us. We're His servants, and yet we're also His sons and daughters.

That indwelling Holy Spirit brings forth fruit in our lives as we yield to Him. But we're exhorted in Ephesians 5:18, to be filled to overflowing with the Holy Spirit. There's a constant overflow He desires for us. This is so the overflow will touch the lives of others.

## THE PRINCIPLE OF DISPLACEMENT

Imagine you had a two-quart plastic container. When you fill it with water and keep pouring water into it, no matter how much more water you pour on top of that, it will never hold more than two quarts; it will overflow. Yes, it contains two quarts of water, but it's overflowing because there's this constant source of water coming upon it.

Now, suppose there are twenty golf balls in that two-quart container. The reality is there aren't two quarts of water in it at all. There are only five cups of water because those twenty golf balls have displaced the water and haven't allowed the container to be completely full.

The point is this: each of those golf balls could represent something which displaces the water of the Holy Spirit in our hearts. Jesus talked about it in the parable of the sower— the deceitfulness of riches, the cares of this world and the desires for other things which choke the word so that it becomes unfruitful.

Let's say that each of those golf balls represent certain issues in our life: personal expectations and demands upon others, hatred, resentment, bigotry, anger, unforgiveness, unbelief, fear, sexual involvement outside of the marriage covenant, adultery, unholiness and impurity, immorality and pornography, idolatry, self-satisfaction at the expense of others, time, money, shutting off the heart from the needs of others, lying, and stealing.

As God deals with us, one by one those golf balls are removed when we yield to Him. We repent of those things; we set those things aside and let them go. Doing so allows us to experience more of His love.

This whole principle of displacement is interesting to me because I believe God wants to work in my life to remove the golf balls so I can contain more of Him. Those things that I'm hanging onto, that I think can fill my life, only displace a deeper measure of what He has for me.

All that's left for us is to ask God to saturate us with His love. It's not reckless abandon on our part; it's the wisest, most natural thing a child of God can do.

Let's fall back upon God's promises like we've never fallen upon them before. God knows our need, and He may allow things to be adjusted and switched around; but He's not going to forsake us. He'll be faithful to His Word. His love for us is so great. Let's become saturated with His love.

MUSICIAN for services is Robert Claycamp shown with his wife Jeanie. Only married couple presently at Shiloh, they expect their first child in January.

From 1970 newspaper article on the Christian house ministry in Aloha, Oregon

# CHAPTER 3

## ~~◎~~ LOVE IS PATIENT ~~◎~~

It had only been a few months since we stood at the altar and proclaimed our vows to one another before God and our wedding guests. We meant every word and were so hopeful. Even though we were only eighteen years old, we believed Christ could see us through anything and everything.

Yet now we found ourselves on the brink of exploding apart in resentment and bitterness. My wife had been pregnant only a few weeks and our living situation was difficult to say the least. We'd joined a Christian youth ministry which had set up communal-style houses in Oregon and California. These houses were live-in discipleship centers for outreach and nightly Bible studies.

The house we were in was a single family residence, two stories with a full basement in a small community west of Portland, Oregon. My wife and I had the one bedroom on the first floor, the two upstairs bedrooms were full of bunk beds where the college-aged girls stayed, and the basement was full of bunk beds for the college-aged boys. There were about twenty of us living there... with one bathroom.

I was so zealous to be a sold-out believer that I gave away many of our wedding gifts for the use of the house without asking my wife. It didn't seem to matter to me at the time. I even signed over our 1964 Volkswagen Beetle to the house ministry. It had been my wife's car before we were married.

My wife felt very alone in the midst of all these people and changes. Even though we were dedicated believers in Christ, zealous to a fault, her dreams for a normal American family living in a little house with a white picket fence and flower beds below the windows were being dashed daily.

She regularly began communicating with her mother about the difficulties, much to my displeasure. "After all," I thought at the time, "we're to leave the world behind and follow Christ."

Ultimately the situation came to a head. I blew up at her and told her that if she wanted to be around her mother so much, I'd pack her bags and send her home. I wanted to serve the Lord without distraction. I drove her to her parents' house and headed back to the Christian commune.

That night the Lord spoke to me very clearly by His Spirit that I hadn't reflected His heart in the situation. I hadn't been patient with my wife. I hadn't understood all she had to deal with. I'd been impetuous and rash in my self-righteousness. I needed to repent to Him and to her.

The next morning I called her at her mother's house. Her mother was at work and she was there alone. I apologized to her over the phone and asked her forgiveness. She began to share with me that her place in life was with me, not with her parents. The calling of God upon my life was to be her calling as well. Somehow we'd make it through all the challenges.

I couldn't believe what I was hearing. God had worked in both of our lives to bring us to the cross of Jesus and die to ourselves. I quickly drove over to her mother's house, picked her up and we came back to the house ministry together. We had humbled ourselves before the Lord and He rescued our marriage, our family, and our future together.

What we learned in this early lesson on patience was this: God's patience with us was of a completely different quality and origin than our patience with one another. Even though we, in our own impatience, had brought about such division in our marriage, God patiently dealt with us over these last forty two years as an expression of His love.

## LONGSUFFERING IS SLOW TO ANGER

The very first characteristic of God's love that Paul pens in verse 4 of 1 Corinthians 13 is patience, or longsuffering as some translations refer to it. What does it mean that God's love is longsuffering? Vine's Expository Dictionary of Biblical Words puts it this way: *"Longsuffering is that quality of self-restraint in the face of provocation which does not hastily retaliate or promptly punish; it is the opposite of anger, and is associated with mercy, and it's used to describe God."*

Thayer's Greek Lexicon describes this word long-suffering: *"To be patient in bearing the offenses and injuries of others; to be mild and slow in avenging; to be longsuffering, slow to anger, slow to punish."*

God's love meekly and patiently bears ill treatment from others. It's patient with others even when spoken against. It gives the other person space, it's willing to wait and it doesn't manipulate or pressure the other person into changing.

Now, isn't that the kind of spouse we want? Isn't that the kind of children we want? Isn't that the kind of parents we want? Isn't that the kind of loving relationships we want?

Why did Paul use the word longsuffering as the first attribute of God's love? There are two reasons I can think of. One has to do with the heart of the Corinthian believers. They were always trying to put themselves forward as being better than the next person by saying, "You might have a word of knowledge; but I speak in tongues. I've even done miracles!"

Paul is in effect saying to them, "Listen; God's love is longsuffering. It doesn't retaliate." God's love was so different in quality than how the Corinthian believers were treating one another, and flaunting their spiritual gifts.

Secondly, remember that the Holy Spirit was inspiring Paul to write these words. This wasn't just a document that some man wrote on his own. We know from the Scriptures that these words were inspired by the Holy Spirit.

Longsuffering starts with God, not with us. It's a description of who He is, first and foremost. In Exodus 34, Moses requested to have God show him His glory. When God did show him His glory He proclaimed His name along with the glory.

Here is what we read in Exodus 34:5-7:

> [5] *Now the LORD descended in the cloud and stood with him there, and proclaimed the name of the LORD.* [6] *And the LORD passed before him and proclaimed, "The LORD, the LORD God, merciful and gracious, longsuffering, and abounding in goodness and truth,* [7] *keeping mercy for thousands, forgiving iniquity and transgression and sin, by no means clearing the guilty, visiting the iniquity of the fathers upon the children and the children's children to the third and the fourth generation."*

## ACTING UNDER IMPULSE

Sometimes it's helpful to take a word and look at the opposite of what it means. What does it look like when we're impatient? We overreact in anger and end up causing great damage, either emotionally or even physically. Acting under impulse or impetuously is a common expression of impatience and leads to regrettable decisions and choices that may not be easily changed.

I believe the most common expression of impatience is anger. It can show its ugly head when our momentum has been interrupted or our plans have been jeopardized. Take a look at road rage, for instance. Why has it become such a problem in our society? It's because somebody's momentum or plan got interrupted. Then this anger rises and regrettable actions follow.

This isn't God's love in action. We know from the Bible that most people's anger is sinful because it's based upon self-orientation.

**James 1:19-20**

*[19] So then, my beloved brethren, let every man be swift to hear, slow to speak, slow to wrath; [20] for the wrath of man does not produce the righteousness of God.*

Having a short fuse is nothing to brag about. It usually, if not always, leads to sinful action. That kind of behavior isn't honorable to God. Not only that, but the trust damage is huge. When we explode into an angry tirade, it's a kind of flesh grenade, an emotional IED (improvised explosive device) in the ground that goes off and body parts are everywhere so to speak—in our marriages, families, and within our other relationships.

Anger may obtain its goal of controlling the outward chaos, but it leaves tremendous soul-shrapnel in others. When God's love rules our hearts, though, sinful anger won't be a byproduct. That's what we want deep down. Anger is a manifestation of an agenda that's self-based, not God-based; it's selfishness at its worst and deceptive at its best.

Impatience wants to retaliate first and ask questions later. It has nothing to do with healing, reconciliation, or restoration. When it comes down to it, impatience is a lack of trusting that God is somehow in control of everything. It doubts God's love for us and the truth of what the Scriptures say about Him and about us. We need to call it what it is— sin. It needs to be owned up to and repented of before God.

## LONGSUFFERING TOWARD YOUR SPOUSE

I think the marriage relationship is one of the best venues to begin letting God's love express itself. Remember that patience, as we're examining it, is an expression of God's love, not merely a human-based patience.

So what's the difference? Human-based patience may be founded upon one's personality and temperament. Some people are more naturally patient than others; but that doesn't mean God's love is flowing through them. It means they have learned to interact well with others and be considerate.

Even though there's this natural patience working with other people, ultimately self is still found at its core. Only the believer in the Lord Jesus Christ can be filled with God's Spirit. The Bible says that God doesn't give His Spirit to the world, but to those who have put their trust in His Son, Jesus (John 14:17). God counts it as very precious that He would take His very Spirit and place Him within the very core of the being of one of His sons and daughters who've trusted His Son.

God's love is unique because it's not humanly manufactured. Can we remember the last time we lashed out at our spouse? Let's ask the Lord to reveal to us why it was so important to deal with the situation the way we did. Was God's love at the heart of our words, our tone of voice, our attitude, and our actions? Or were we just ticked off that our plans and ideas were disrupted?

How do we start again with our spouses? We own up to our impatience, that it was sinful, that we were walking according to the flesh and not according to the Spirit of God. We ask them to forgive us for not honoring and loving them—and really mean it.

We shouldn't demand they ask our forgiveness for their sinful words, tone, and actions. It's not our place to do so; it's the Holy Spirit's responsibility to bring them there. We need to make sure we're personally accountable to God by asking Him to change us from the inside out. We can also ask Him to do the same for our spouses. This week, as a challenge to us all, let's ask the Lord to fill us with His love. Let's ask Him to help us have a mind set of patience, longsuffering, and how to wait for further information before reacting. Self-control is one of the byproducts of God's love as seen in Galatians 5:23. I'm not saying our marriage relationships are going to change overnight. It could get worse because our spouse might start thinking we're turning into some holier-than-thou person. It may be that they'll test us just to see if it's real or not. But we need to continue to do it so we can maintain a strong relationship with the Lord. In turn, our actions will begin to bless them because God will use it for His glory.

As husbands, we have the responsibility of sanctifying our lives for the sake of our spouses. As wives, we have the responsibility before the Lord to sanctify our lives to affect our husbands. As parents, we have the responsibility to sanctify our lives because our children are going to be affected, either for good or for evil.

## LONGSUFFERING TOWARD THE FAMILY

Let's consider another application with the family. Many times we fall back upon habits and behaviors that were the environment of our homes when we were growing up. We can look back and identify them as either productive and healthy, or harsh, even abusive.

And unless we put God's love into full control of our lives, our soul's patterns of sinful actions, reactions, and emotional settings may begin to come out over time. We can then easily default back to what feels more natural to us, even though it's wrong and sinful in God's eyes.

As parents we raise our children to be oriented to our order of things, not vice versa. A child-centered home is a chaotic home in my opinion. Children need structure; they need the correction and security of parents who are in charge of the overall direction of the family. It doesn't mean that parents should be drill sergeants or oppressive; the Scriptures warn fathers not to provoke their children to wrath.

**Ephesians 6:4** *And you, fathers, do not provoke your children to wrath, but bring them up in the training and admonition of the Lord.*

This Scripture implies structure, correction, and security. We also see this counsel in the book of Colossians:

**Colossians 3:21** *Fathers, do not provoke your children, lest they become discouraged.*

This Scripture advises us to not crush the child's spirit in our efforts to discipline them. Sometimes when we as parents are under pressure to get to a certain destination at a certain time, we expect our children to have the same sense of urgency we do. We find they shape up for a moment and then get distracted by the dog, the toy, the shoes that don't fit right, or something else. Meanwhile, time is ticking away and the impatience is morphing into a real monster inside us. Our voice is now at one hundred decibels, and the redness in our face is evident.

That's when our children don't look us in the eye, but they obey because they've learned through our not-so-subtle training that when these things get to nuclear levels, it's best to go along with it.

The problem with this whole scenario is that we're training them when to obey. In their little minds, they're waiting for the needle to get to that one point and then they go, "Okay, action time." But the responsibility comes back to us as parents; we didn't include the reality that our children don't think like adults.

Dawdling is a good word to describe how children are in terms of time limits. We want them to get ready quickly, but then we find them on the stairs, picking their nose; and we say, "What? Come on, we're so late. What are you doing? You're making me late, you're making me look bad." Now we're getting to the core of the issue. You are making **me** look bad. See, it's all coming back to self-orientation. We didn't think ahead to what was going to be required to get these little ones ready in time.

Let's say we're on the way to church and we've gotten off to a late start. We're driving down the freeway, and our children start bickering in the back seat. Then we start swinging our arms behind us to reach them and stop the bickering. The entire scene in the car has turned into chaos.

But when we pull into the church parking lot we tell all the occupants in the car, "Quiet down, quiet down. Okay everybody, here we go." We walk right into church and say, "Praise the Lord, it's such a good day."

Here's the reality. We probably left the house too late in the first place. To get to church by 9:00 o'clock on Sunday morning, we're going to have to start at 6:30 a.m. Maybe we can get away with frequently blowing up at our children when they're very young; but unless we change those patterns, we're going to create some real resentment in our children for how we've dealt with them. Relationships with our children are likely to become distant, and that's not what we want as parents.

This all stems from not letting God's love flow through our lives. Unless we let God work in us in this area, we'll tend to set patterns in their lives for how they'll deal with their children when they aren't walking in the Spirit of God.

So, how do we start again with our families in this area of longsuffering and exhibiting God's patience? It's similar to what was mentioned with the marriage application. First of all, we need to own up to our own sinful responses before God and ask for His help. It goes something like this: "God, You're longsuffering, and I need that quality in my life so the overflow can minister to my family." Then, we should sit the children down and ask their forgiveness for how we've dealt with things no matter who was wrong.

What about us showing love to our parents? Maybe their age has limited them in understanding all that we have to deal with in our jobs and families. Maybe we've been extremely impatient with them because they're becoming more and more of a burden to our plans, momentum, and goals. Listen very carefully to me: dishonoring our parents is dishonoring God. God puts a high value on honoring our parents. It doesn't mean we do everything they say, but it has to be a choice on our part to honor them.

What we're seeking to address here is living out God's love through being patient and longsuffering toward our children and parents, and seeing them as God sees them. If we don't have a strategy in dealing with our children and parents in this way, then it's time to ask God for His strategy for us and to turn things around.

## LONGSUFFERING TOWARD OTHERS

Finally, in considering all other relationships, God has called us to walk in His love toward all people. The first expression of that love should be patience. Yet when people treat us harshly, what's our reaction? I think that's the part we have to bring to God saying, "Lord, help me to understand what's going on. Why are they dealing with me in this way? What's going on in their life that makes them react to these kinds of things?"

It's not that we have to become a psychologist to understand why they do everything they do. It's that we need to take it to the Lord and say, "You know God, I can't control what they do, but I can ask You to help me respond in a way that reflects You instead of me." Jesus said we're to bless those who curse us, do good to those who do evil toward us, pray for those who despitefully use us and persecute us (Matthew 5:44); and the sole foundation for this is because that's how God dealt with us. So we're to respond to others with God's love.

God has been patient and longsuffering with us. He'll continue to be this way forever because it's His nature. This attribute is an expression of His love. God is waiting to fill us to overflowing with His love so that true, godly longsuffering can flow out from us to a needy world.

Alta, Elmer, Beverly, and newborn Robert

# CHAPTER 4

## ～≥ LOVE IS KIND ～≥

Kansas, 1938. They met at their local high school and had waited patiently to get married. He had to work his way through high school because of his mother's blindness and his father's poverty, eventually graduating at age twenty-two. She was one of the daughters of the local preacher; a bubbly, spiritually sensitive young lass.

Just before they were married she was in a terrible car accident that damaged her brain. It led to grand mal epilepsy that showed up after they married. The two lived in her parents' home for the first year or so. He began attending Bible college at his father-in-law's encouragement. He wanted to be a preacher like him.

The time came for him to occasionally step in and preach on Sunday mornings at some of the local churches. While he'd be speaking, his beloved wife would sometimes have an epileptic seizure. He then had to stop speaking and go down to the front row and take care of her until she was somewhat back on track. Afterwards, he'd get back up to the pulpit and try to continue from where he'd left off.

After a few of these incidents, people began to complain to the district supervisor of the denomination. He was called in and told that because of his wife's condition he'd have to seek a different vocation. Although he was crushed over the whole situation, he knew that the pressure on her would be too great. So he left preaching and entered schooling to become a teacher.

That was the picture of my parents' first years of marriage. My earliest recollections of them are mental snapshots watching my father care for my mother in her malady. The common medicine used to lessen those seizures during those years was Phenobarbital. It may have slowed things a bit for her but never reduced those seizures for more than a week or two. My father's care for her in public and private was the same: kindness and understanding. While some in public were put off and even appalled by her actions while having an epileptic seizure, he embraced her as if it were his own malady... which in effect it was. She died in 1967 from cancer. She was a devout believer in the Lord Jesus Christ. I'll get to fellowship with her forever when I go home to be with the Lord.

## KINDNESS IS AN OUTWARD EXPRESSION OF GOD'S LOVE

While longsuffering and patience are love's inner strength, kindness is one of the first outward expressions of God's love. There's a kindness that humans are capable of expressing without even drawing upon the Holy Spirit. We all can naturally recognize a kind act done toward us or another person. This action of kindness is simply an expression of our being created in the image of God.

But there are differences between human kindness and God's kindness. It has to do with the origin and the end goal. Human kindness brings one a self-satisfaction and is its own reward. But divine kindness, the kindness that springs from God's love alone, ends with the desire to glorify God and His truth, and to point others to Him. It flows out of remembering how God has been kind to us.

God's kindness looks for a way to be constructive in the midst of our circumstances. Understand though that God's kindness doesn't equate with weakness. We may think being kind means we have to be a doormat or have no backbone. But this is not the case if we look at the definition of kindness.

The Hebrew word for lovingkindness is *chesed* (*khesed'*). This is a word that combines strength, steadfastness, and love. These words are inseparably linked together. Webster's 1828 Dictionary defines kindness in this way: *"Disposed to do good to others and to make them happy by granting their requests, supplying their wants or assisting them in distress; having tenderness or goodness of nature; benevolent."*

Kenneth Wuest, in his commentary on the Greek language in the New Testament, defines the word used for kind as follows: *"Gentle, benign, pervading and penetrating the whole nature, mellowing all which would have been harsh and austere."*

Here are a few Scriptures that mention the lovingkindness of God. The Bible contains additional words that are interchangeable with the word kind such as goodness, gentleness, and graciousness. All these are part of that quality of kindness.

**Psalm 40:10** *I have not hidden Your righteousness within my heart; I have declared Your faithfulness and Your salvation; I have not concealed Your lovingkindness and Your truth From the great assembly.*

I like the combination of lovingkindness and truth here. Sometimes we can be so focused on making sure our doctrine is right that we leave off showing lovingkindness. On the other hand, we can be so fixed on showing lovingkindness that we compromise biblical truth.

**Psalm 103:4** *Who redeems your life from destruction, Who crowns you with lovingkindness and tender mercies,*

Psalm 103 is a description of the Lord's benefits to us. He crowns us with lovingkindness and tender mercies. It's like He's setting it right on our heads as a crown. It's as if the Lord is saying, "This is something I want you to experience, it's something I want you to understand: how I cherish you!" It's a unilateral action on His part.

**Psalm 143:8** *Cause me to hear Your lovingkindness in the morning, For in You do I trust; Cause me to know the way in which I should walk, For I lift up my soul to You.*

Some of us may be going through very challenging times right now. Maybe it's because of the economy or something else going on in our lives. The Lord wants to give us His strategy, but it's one step at a time. He doesn't usually give us step two until we take step one. Even though we don't see what is going to happen afterwards, we have to at least take step one. We have to step out in faith.

**Jeremiah 31:3** *The LORD has appeared of old to me, saying: "Yes, I have loved you with an everlasting love; Therefore with lovingkindness I have drawn you."*

Those of us who've trusted Christ for our salvation know that He drew us with His lovingkindness in the first place. It was a purposed action on His part.

**Isaiah 54:8** *"With a little wrath I hid my face from you for a moment; But with everlasting kindness I will have mercy on you," Says the LORD, your Redeemer."*

Some of us may have walked away from the Lord for a while. We may think we've crossed the line of no return with God. But God wants us back. His Son bore our sin. The Scripture in Isaiah 54 says, *With everlasting kindness I will have mercy on you, says the LORD, your Redeemer.* Yes, there are repercussions we'll have to deal with if we wander away; but He'll be with us because He's in it for the long haul.

## THE OPPOSITE OF KINDNESS

Let's look at some of the antonyms of kindness: inconsiderate, mean-spirited, cruel, abusive, and harsh. To say that we're abiding in God's love, and yet deal with others in a harsh, critical, abusive, belittling, or cruel way is hypocrisy and self-deception.

The Corinthian believers weren't treating one another with kindness.

**1 Corinthians 3:3** *for you are still carnal. For where there are envy, strife and divisions among you, are you not carnal and behaving like mere men?*

You can go through this list of love's attributes in 1 Corinthians 13:4-8, and apply it right to the Corinthian believers. This is especially obvious when the apostle Paul gets into the descriptions of what God's love does NOT look like. They were in Christ, yes, but they weren't choosing to walk in the Spirit and in God's love.

Many people say they believe in God's love, but often they are so very unkind in how they deal with others. This is seen when someone ignores them, crosses them, or offends them. Somehow they think when that happens, they're justified in letting loose a barrage of vengeful, spiteful tirades and threats. It doesn't matter to them if it grieves the Holy Spirit. "After all," they say, "look what they said or did to me." I've observed this sinful tendency in marriages, I've watched it in families, and, sad to say, I've even seen it within churches. As long as people are nice to one another, there aren't many problems. As long as they're happy, everything is fine; but as soon as they're crossed, man, head behind the couch. All of the sudden they're the most vengeful person, and they'll cut that person off, never talk to them again, and hold the grudge for years.

One can learn more about the depth of a Christian's character by how they react when they're mistreated than by the many good works they may seem to do. People do good works for many reasons, some of which are totally motivated by the flesh for self-glory, self-satisfaction, and as a means to try to work off their guilt.

But true godly kindness will be a natural outflow when we walk in God's love. No matter how long those sinful habits have been yielded to, God can change things in an instant; but we have to own up to our sin and say, "God, I haven't been a person of kindness in my marriage or in my other relationships. Please work within me by the Holy Spirit."

## KINDNESS IN MARRIAGE

For those of us who are married, think back to when we first met our spouse. We thought about how to be kind when we got together. If we had a disagreement, we said to ourselves, "Okay, how can I really show kindness here?" We worked on it, and our relationship consumed our thoughts because it was all so fresh and new; we found ways to express it.

Then once we became comfortable with each other, the guard began to drop. There were those offenses that came out, little disrespectful tones of voice. Then we found those acts of kindness began to appear less and less, and walls built up. When we're genuinely kind toward our spouses, it makes it so much easier for them to love and trust us. But when we're not kind, when we're critical, abusive, harsh, mean-spirited, or demeaning, do we think that's going to foster closeness between us? No, it tears down our relationships; it's destructive. Kindness builds trust; harshness, cruelty, disrespect, dishonor, and abusiveness destroy trust.

Think back on the past week with our spouses. In what ways might we have been unkind, harsh, critical, maybe even condescending to them? When was the last time we actually showed a special act of kindness to them? I'm not talking about being kind so we can lead up to intimacy. I'm talking about kindness that's genuinely kind because God has been so kind to us.

It may be time to ask our spouses to forgive us for not walking in the love of God, especially as it's expressed in kindness. Forgiveness begins with owning up to our sins, humbling ourselves, and asking forgiveness of the one we've offended. There's no other way our relationships are going to get back on track until we take those steps.

On the other hand, if our spouses have shown kindness toward us, we need to reinforce that in them. If we desire to have those actions happen more often, we need to encourage the other person. It's not flattery to do this, it's affirming. God desires that we affirm the things that are right in the other person. Flattery is when we're doing it for selfish motives to get something for ourselves, to build them up so we can use it to manipulate them later.

## KINDNESS IN THE FAMILY

What about kindness shown in the family? I believe one of the most basic requirements to guard in any family is honor and respect between its members. When unkind actions are allowed without dealing with them, resentments build up, disrespect grows, conflicts increase, and fights break out. When someone is raised in an abusive family, it's often hard for them to handle kindness shown to them by others. They have difficulty trusting it. The only kindness they can relate to is the lack of abuse. There's no positive action of kindness they've regularly experienced.

So as they grew up, when somebody was actually kind to them, it was an awkward feeling for them because they weren't used to it. They're drawn to the display of kindness, but tend to sabotage it to prove it wasn't genuine. After all, it was how it ended up anyway in their past experiences. So they kind of poke and test, poke and test. Finally, the person breaks down out of exasperation, and they say, "I thought it was like that", because they didn't know what to do with it.

God wants to refashion our hearts to understand His kindness to us so He can change us from the inside out. If we grew up in an abusive home, we have the ability as a Christian to break that chain of abuse so it doesn't continue on to our children; but it's going to be hard. We're the ones who are going to have to consciously work on it and ask God for His help to break that chain of abuse.

God is a healer and He can heal our souls. *He heals the broken-hearted and binds up their wounds* as it says in Psalm 147:3, but we have to stand in the gap. We have to stop that pattern of abuse right here with us and not extend it into the next generation.

God's kindness must be allowed to flow among each and every family member— between the siblings, and between the parents and children alike. It's one thing to get children to interact in kindness toward one another; it's another thing for parents to act in kindness toward their children. What happens when our children misbehave? Do we continue to act in kindness? In Christ, we have His strength, steadfastness, and love as a threefold cord to help us.

Our children are going to naturally test our rules. That's how they find their boundaries. We might say to them, "I need you to pick up your toys," and they could respond, "I don't feel like it." They're testing those limits, albeit maybe subconsciously. God wants us to be kind when we're challenged by our children. How are we to show that kindness? We have to be filled with God's love to be able to do that, and we have to understand that the ability to do it comes from the Lord's power.

God's kindness is an everlasting and infinite kindness. He's put His kindness in us by means of the Holy Spirit. But we have to do things His way. Can we discipline our children in kindness? Absolutely! The opposite of kindness is not acceptable when we discipline our children. Harshness, belittling them, and being condescending to them are destructive efforts.

We as parents set patterns in their little hearts on how they'll deal with their children when they grow up. We've got to break the chain of wrong habits right now, and let God's kindness rule in our lives. Let's choose to walk in the power and love of the Holy Spirit, let Him rebuild our families and let His kindness be the rule of our households.

## KINDNESS TO ALL PEOPLE

What does God's kindness look like in the rest of our relationships? God has called us to be His children, and we're to be known as bearers of His love. We're called to walk in love toward all people, whether they're Christians or not. As a matter of fact, it's especially needful to treat those who don't know the Lord yet with His kindness.

Maybe we've been unkind to the bank teller, the grocery clerk, to our fellow employee, or to the cashier. Maybe the mechanic messed up our car so we feel like saying, "You know what? I'm just going to dump the hopper on them, that'll show them. They'll never treat anybody bad again like they treated me." All of the sudden we've shifted gears and we're in the flesh. We can't say that we're being guided by the Holy Spirit with that attitude.

When we make a choice to live out God's kindness each day with all the people we meet, then when we do slip up, we'll go back to those we've sinned against, apologize, and ask their forgiveness. We've been called to reflect His heart to the world around us.

Here's an assignment for us for the next week: take today and the following six days and purpose to be kind to our spouses, families, to people we interact with, even to the driver that happens to cut us off on the freeway. Let's keep our hands on the steering wheel and say, "You know God, I've probably done that to somebody else."

Remember, God's kindness is the first expression of God's love.

# CHAPTER 5

## ~~~ LOVE DOES NOT ENVY ~~~

We had worked so hard at building up our congregation over those first ten years. Starting out as a small home Bible study, it had grown to about 250 families. But now, all that was beginning to dwindle away.

Another church in our association of churches had been started just down the road. There was no doubt in my mind as to the hand of God upon that pastor and his congregation. Their church was growing by leaps and bounds. It was an exciting time for them. They were faithfully teaching God's Word. Many were coming to Christ at each of their services. The school in which they were meeting was becoming too small to handle the crowds.

The pastor called me and asked if I knew of any facilities that might be available to meet their needs. At that moment the Holy Spirit nudged my heart to give him the contact of the shopping center we'd been negotiating with about a mile away. We still had a year and a half left on our current lease anyway.

At first I resisted the prompting. "After all," I thought, "this is our opportunity to really grow." But immediately a sense of rightness came over me and I gave the pastor the contact.

This pastor is a good friend of mine. Deep down I wanted to see him flourish and be as fruitful in Christ as he could be. But I was not ready for the schooling I had just entered.

As they signed the contract to lease and later purchase that shopping center for their ministry, the excitement surrounding the move spilled over to many in our own congregation. Friends contacted friends. Folks from our church began to attend their services and made decisions to become members there.

Our numbers were dwindling and the finances were shrinking. I had to lay off most of my staff and was considering a part-time job to make ends meet. On top of it all, because of the closeness of the shopping center to our church, I was driving by it twice a day.

Resentment began building in my heart as I passed by. I remember saying to the Lord, "This isn't fair. How come they get all the blessings and we're stuck in our situation?" It was then that the Holy Spirit convicted my heart of jealousy, envy, and covetousness over another man's ministry. It surprised me that I could have those thoughts and feelings. I knew they were sinful, but I just couldn't stop the flow of anger.

When I cried out to the Lord for His strategy on how to be freed from my septic heart, this directive came to me in the car: "I want you to pray for their church every time you drive by it. I don't want you to take a different way to the office to avoid seeing it.   Also, I want you to stop in once a week and rejoice with them as they build out their facility."

I couldn't believe it. You've got to be kidding! But deep down I knew that the only way to overcome these feelings of jealousy, envy and covetousness was to head straight into it with His power, grace and courage.

So for the next year I obeyed, albeit reluctantly at first. But as the weeks went by I found that little by little the Holy Spirit was washing my heart and helping me to see things from Christ's perspective. By the time they moved into their facility I felt free of the jealousy and envy, truly rejoicing in their new facility.

We made it through that time as a church. We ended up moving our congregation about eight miles east of them. The next twenty years were full of blessings and fruitfulness for us and for the other church by the grace of God.

## THE DIFFERENCE BETWEEN JEALOUSY, ENVY, AND COVETOUSNESS

Jealousy, envy, and covetousness can captivate us as Christians and render us fruitless. But God's love can flush out selfishness and narrow mindedness and replace them with such grace.

As we're examining the attributes of God's love in 1 Corinthians 13 we come to what God's love is not—God's love *does not envy.* Let's include jealously and covetousness with this word envy because I think there are subtle aspects that need to be understood with each one. God's love has nothing to do with envy, jealously, or covetousness.

Some have defined envy as a feeling of discontentment or resentful longing aroused by someone else's possessions, qualities, or opportunities.

Merriam-Webster's Dictionary defines envy this way: "The painful or resentful awareness of an advantage enjoyed by another jointed with a desire to possess the same advantage."

Here is another definition of envy: "An emotion that occurs when a person lacks another's perceived superior quality or achievement, or possession, and either desires it or wishes that the other person lacked it."

So envy includes the idea that 'I want what you have, and I don't want you to have it.' Envy has that little twist right at the end. Envy typically involves two people, but jealously usually includes three people. Jealousy is that fear of losing something one possesses to another person. Envy is the pain or frustration caused by another person having something that one doesn't have. Do you see the slight difference? To envy another is to feel ill will, jealousy, or discontentment at his possession of something that one keenly desires to have or achieve oneself.

Let's include one more word: covetousness. To covet is to ardently and wrongfully long for something that belongs to another person. It's more of a general term. Covetousness is like the umbrella under which envy and jealously hide. When you read through the epistle of 1 Corinthians, all the things Paul was writing here in chapter 13 specifically addressed their problems. *Love does not envy* would apply to them because they were envious of each other's spiritual gifts and advantages. There were divisions over who had been their discipler, who had the most powerful gifts, and who had the most captivating presentation. Paul had all of these issues on his heart before he set his pen to parchment.

As Paul began to address the truth about spiritual gifts, all he could think about was the bickering, the hassle, and the one-upmanship that was going on within the church. It was almost as if he wrote chapter 12, then put his pen down and thought, "I have to go to the heart of this whole thing." Then he wrote chapter 13, after which he went on and instructed them on how the particular spiritual gifts of tongues and prophecy should be exercised within a congregational setting.

God's love has no selfish envy in any way. The goal of His love is to enrich the object of that love and to rejoice when blessings are poured out upon another. It doesn't consider its own status, standing, or circumstance in relation to the one being benefited.

Envy is sin; there's no other way to say it. God desires to flush out those motions of sin by the power of the Holy Spirit when we call upon Him to do so. God is ready to work, but we have to invite Him to work. If we walk in the Spirit we will not fulfill the lusts of the flesh as Galatians 5:16 says.

When we're going through difficult times, whether it's in our marriages, families, or our relationships with others, it's easy to become envious at others' situations because of what hasn't happened in our lives.

We can pretend that envy doesn't bother us, but we have to own up to it sooner or later. We have to face it squarely, and then take it to the Lord because only He can give us the victory. Usually the victory comes when we do something in faith to push against it. That's why Jesus said to *"bless those who curse you, and pray for those who spitefully use you"* (Luke 6:28). This puts us into an active mode to present it before the Lord on a regular basis. If we just ignore it and pretend it's not there, the thing is like a weed and it grows and spreads. I guarantee it'll turn into bitterness.

When we're going through difficult times in our marriages, families, or our relationships with others, it's easy to be envious of others' situations. We can say, "Why do they get all the breaks? Why do they get all the benefits and have a nice home, car, job, etc? Why do I always have things fall apart around me?"

When these kinds of thoughts are going through our minds, understand, first of all, that our eyes are on ourselves. We've become the standard of what's right and fair instead of having the Lord Jesus in our focus. Secondly, by this kind of attitude we're actually accusing God of being unfair when it comes to our situation. It's just our own unbelief in His promises to us, and we're subtly setting ourselves up as judge and jury against God Himself. The question that we should be asking God is, "Why can't I rejoice in pure joy when another brother or sister is advantaged?"

Why is it that we're envious of a marriage that's doing well when ours is in the tank? It's because of the sin that dwells in our flesh. We need to offer a plea to God for His grace and mercy to change what ails us on the inside. God is a gracious God and He knows the full story.

## EXAMPLES OF ENVY IN SCRIPTURE

Let's look at some examples of envy in Scripture. I think we have to start with the very first sinner, Satan himself, called Lucifer in the Bible. When we examine the Bible cover to cover, we'll not find an exact record of how Lucifer sinned from the beginning. But there are references here and there. There are also some veiled references that can be found in the books of Isaiah and Ezekiel.

In Isaiah, while prophesying to the King of Babylon, there's an overreaching prophetic word to the highest example of pride and subsequent fall of the devil himself. Of course, the prophecy is directed to the King of Babylon initially; but to summarize this king's heart of pride, the Lord, through Isaiah, brings forward the ultimate king of pride and what happened to him (referring to Satan).

**Isaiah 14:12-15**
*12 "How you are fallen from heaven, O Lucifer, son of the morning! How you are cut down to the ground, You who weakened the nations! 13 For you have said in your heart: 'I will ascend into heaven, I will exalt my throne above the stars of God; I will also sit on the mount of the congregation On the farthest sides of the north; 14 I will ascend above the heights of the clouds, I will be like the Most High.' 15 Yet you shall be brought down to Sheol, To the lowest depths of the Pit."*

That's called envy. Prophetically, Isaiah was drawing upon the king of pride, Lucifer, the one who first sinned in order to describe the coming fall of the King of Babylon.

Then, in the book of Ezekiel, while addressing the king of Tyre, we find the same overreaching prophecy drawing upon Satan as one who had the highest of privileges, yet how his own pride led to his downfall.

**Ezekiel 28:11-15**

*[11] Moreover the word of the LORD came to me, saying, [12] "Son of man, take up a lamentation for the king of Tyre, and say to him, 'Thus says the Lord GOD: "You were the seal of perfection, Full of wisdom and perfect in beauty. [13] You were in Eden, the garden of God; Every precious stone was your covering: The sardius, topaz, and diamond, Beryl, onyx, and jasper, Sapphire, turquoise, and emerald with gold. The workmanship of your timbrels and pipes Was prepared for you on the day you were created. [14] "You were the anointed cherub who covers; I establish you; You were on the holy mountain of God; You walked back and forth in the midst of fiery stones. [15] You were perfect in your ways from the day you were created, Till iniquity was found in you. [16] "By the abundance of your trading You became filled with violence within, And you sinned; Therefore I cast you as a profane thing Out of the mountain of God; And I destroyed you, O covering cherub, from the midst of the fiery stones. [17] "Your heart was lifted up because of your beauty; You corrupted your wisdom for the sake of your splendor; I cast you to the ground, I laid you before kings That they might gaze at you."'"*

Let me give you a little illustration of how these prophecies can be seen as ultimately applying to Satan. Let's say you were sitting in an auditorium looking at the stage. The curtain in front of you is a sheer curtain with the stage lit behind it. On your side of the curtain is the king of Babylon and the king of Tyre in all their splendor, glory, pomp, and circumstance. But behind the sheer curtain is Satan himself, as it's described there in Isaiah and Ezekiel. That's the idea that's going on in these prophecies. The same heart that was ruling the kings of Babylon and Tyre had ruled Satan and led to his downfall. The first example of envy between humans would be Cain and Abel.

**Genesis 4:3-8**

*³ And in the process of time it came to pass that Cain brought an offering of the fruit of the ground to the LORD. ⁴ Abel also brought of the firstborn of his flock and of their fat. And the LORD respected Abel and his offering, ⁵ But He did not respect Cain and his offering. And Cain was very angry, and his countenance fell. ⁶ So the LORD said to Cain, "Why are you angry? And why has your countenance fallen? ⁷ "If you do well, will you not be accepted? And if you do not do well, sin lies at the door. And its desire is for you, but you should rule over it." ⁸ Now Cain talked with Abel his brother; and it came to pass, when they were in the field, that Cain rose up against Abel his brother and killed him.*

That occurred as the result of envy. Although the text doesn't say it, I personally believe they brought their sacrifices to the entrance of the Garden of Eden by the angels who had the flaming swords to keep them from entering the garden. The Garden of Eden was the place where their parents previously had fellowship with God before everything fell apart. So it was possible they were giving their offerings there to the Lord, and the Lord accepting Abel's offering. Abel was following the pattern that God gave when God slew the animal to give coats of skins to Adam and Eve to cover their nakedness. Cain was just offering his own works from the ground.

LOVE DOES NOT ENVY      63

John the Apostle talks about this in his first general epistle:

**1 John 3:11-15**
*[11] For this is the message that you heard from the beginning, that we should love one another, [12] not as Cain who was of the wicked one and murdered his brother. And why did he murder him? Because his works were evil and his brother's righteous. [13] Do not marvel, my brethren, if the world hates you. [14] We know that we have passed from death to life, because we love the brethren. He who does not love his brother abides in death. [15] Whoever hates his brother is a murderer, and you know that no murderer has eternal life abiding in him.*

There are so many Scriptures that talk about envy. For example, Proverbs 14:30 says, *A sound heart is life to the body, But envy is rottenness to the bones.*

Do we realize what it does to us when our lives are filled with envy? It drains us of energy, it saps us of life, it just eats us up.

In James 4:1-2, the Amplified Version draws out some of the definitions of the words used in the original Greek language.

**James 4:1-2**
*[1] What leads to strife (discord and feuds) {and} how do conflicts (quarrels and fightings) originate among you? Do they not arise from your sensual desires that are ever warring in your bodily members? [2] You are jealous {and} covet [what others have] and your desires go unfulfilled; [so] you become murderers. [To hate is to murder as far as your hearts are concerned.] You burn with envy {and} anger and are*

*not able to obtain [the gratification, the contentment, and the happiness that you seek], so you fight and war. You do not have, because you do not ask.*

## WHAT ENVY DOES TO A MARRIAGE

When envy, jealousy, and covetousness get into our hearts as a married couple, our relationship will come under tremendous pressure and begin to unravel. Sure we're under a marriage covenant, but we're two human beings. Relationship is what marriage is all about.

When we give place to covetousness, jealousy, or envy, they start to rule the heart. Things go from bad to worse. If left unchecked the marriage will fail and the devil will win. If it's caught in time, the Holy Spirit is able to heal hearts, to restore, and to renew. But understand it's going to take time. It's also going to take conscious steps of faith on a daily basis; it's going to take trusting the Lord to heal that deepest part of our souls.

When envy is allowed to rule the heart within a marriage, the focus is so selfish that no blessing which comes our way is good enough. Our spouse finally gives up trying to please us. It's almost like a black hole which absorbs everything that comes close to it.

When jealousy rises up in our hearts, know it's based in selfishness and insecurity. Rather than releasing all of life's situations and circumstances to the Lord's care, His direction and provision, everything is looked upon as a threat to us.

There may have been situations, even traumas that have occurred in our lives where things were stolen from us, things were ripped off from us, even relationships we had with others were broken. It leaves a scar on our hearts and that scar is still there. The memory of what happened is still fresh and there's insecurity that something else is going to happen.

We have to take those things before the Lord because they'll destroy and ultimately undermine our current and new relationships. The Lord can heal us; the Lord can take and bring us into a settledness, a place of security. It's called peace that surpasses all understanding. Unless we take those hurts to the Lord, we're always going to be thinking someone is after our stuff, whether it's our position at work, our possessions, or whatever else we feel threatens us. It almost becomes conspiratorial in nature. All of a sudden, we're looking for some scheme behind every rock.

Can God remove our captivity to jealousy? Yes, He absolutely can. Does it mean we'll never have a twinge of jealousy from now on? Will we be through with fighting for the rest of our lives? No, we'll need to recognize there'll always be a kind of twinge inside us concerning those things. But we can have tremendous victory if jealousy has ruled our lives before.

Will it be easy? Absolutely not; it'll probably be one of the hardest things we've ever had to conquer because it goes deep into who we are and touches our identity. We have to go to the root of the issue and not just cut away branches.

What about covetousness in marriage? As was mentioned earlier, when envy, jealousy, and covetousness rule our hearts, it puts tremendous pressure upon our marriages. When we start feeling trapped, it becomes a kind of seedbed for an affair to happen. All of the sudden, we discover somebody else who just accepts us for who we are and they don't put any pressure on us.

Soon, an emotional enmeshing takes place. Then we start deriving our sense of purpose and fulfillment from this other relationship instead of from our spouse. For the sake of our marriages, we need to get a handle on this and turn from it with the Lord's help.

Let's take the pressure off our marriages. Let's ask God to bring a contentment into our hearts. If we see a discontentment in our spouse, just pray for them. When we pray, ask the Lord to intervene. When He does, they'll begin to be dealt with from all kinds of angles.

## WHAT ENVY DOES TO A FAMILY

As parents, it's our responsibility to help our children understand that envy, jealousy, and covetousness are enemies of the Spirit-filled life. When their friends get certain toys or clothing that we can't afford, we should resist the temptation to rush out and get those same items for them. Instead, it's time for a lesson.

If our children come home and say, "They got those awesome shoes, and I got these stupid bargain store sneakers; it's not fair, dad. How come I always get these hand-me-downs? My brother had these before me."

Now is the time to teach them about blessings and focus. But if our hearts as parents aren't in the right place spiritually, we're going to transfer down to them those same troubles we're fighting with. If our children don't get all that we never had when we were growing up, it's not the end of the world. So much of this transference goes on when we want to live our lives vicariously through our children.

Maybe we just couldn't hit that ball in our P.E. class. We were always the one that got picked last for teams. But now this child of ours is so athletic because our wife came from an athletic background. We're going, "Yeah, all right. He's on first string, you know." Be very careful of the lure to live vicariously through our children. We need to help our children have a biblical world-view, encouraging them to learn how to deal with peer pressure in the way that God wants to help them. Set reasonable boundaries of expenses.

Help them to develop a prayer list of items that they would like to have. Then have them present that list to the Lord. We had to do this in our family because we had three boys and little money. As they were going through high school, they would watch most of their friends get all this fancy stuff, and we didn't have the funds. So we said, "Tell you what. We have $15 for athletic shoes, and the shoes you want are about $85. You pray for the Lord to bring in the difference in the price, and then you can buy those shoes." Actually, we secretly thought that would end the whole matter, but the strangest things would happen. They'd get these little side jobs, and they'd come up with the money. The Lord was wanting to work down at their level to teach them about His heart, the power of prayer, and trusting Him.

As parents, we're to show our children that we're to go to God with the needs we have. They need to understand the difference between wants and needs. Let's bring real life into it for them. We're not protecting them when we merely dish out the money at every whim. This is all part of godly training. It'll help them deal with covetousness, envying, and jealousy in their future.

## WHAT ENVY DOES TO OUR RELATIONSHIPS WITH OTHERS

What does this look like in the rest of our relationships? If we see someone get blessed with something we've wanted for a long time, God has called us to rejoice with them. Their blessing is God's business.

It's interesting to watch how our feelings change toward someone after they've been benefitted in some way. There's this temptation to treat them differently. We tend to want to distance ourselves from them.

But the problem is not with them. The issue is our own envy over their acquisition. When those feelings rise to the surface it's imperative that we deal with it right then and there. If left unchecked, it'll grow into a captivity which will end up isolating us. God is waiting to work in us and through us every day in every way. When we find envy is in our hearts, He's able to flush it out and fill us with His love. All He desires is our humble invitation.

We're called to have God's love toward others, and to rejoice when others are blessed. But we're also to stop when someone else is hurting, come alongside them and weep with them. May the love of God which expresses itself in contentment saturate our hearts today.

# CHAPTER 6

## ~~ LOVE IS NOT SELF-CENTERED ~~

He was the most selfish person I'd ever met. From the moment we came into contact with each other, every word had to do with his world, his ideas, his plans and his agenda. It was all I could do to keep my mouth shut and my attitude in check.

I tried to distance myself from him as best I could, but he kept showing up at the most inappropriate times. How does this guy know my schedule? When he'd see me he'd talk loudly as if I was his best friend and we'd known each other for ages.

How do I get rid of this fellow? The only answer is to put him to death. Yes, you heard me. Kill him. You see, that person is my flesh, my sinful nature. It's selfish through and through.

When I surrendered my life to Christ, the Holy Spirit began to gradually show me how my old life of sin was completely surrendered to selfish ways. Even good deeds had a selfish goal. *O wretched man that I am! Who will deliver me from this body of death? I thank God—though Jesus Christ our Lord!* (Romans 7:24-25).

All of us are accustomed to walking in selfishness, but walking in God's love is something that's especially needful for the believer. It's how others will know we're His disciples.

Let's take a look at the next four attributes of God's love. They're found in 1 Corinthians 13, verses 4 and 5: *Love does not parade itself, is not puffed up, does not behave rudely, and does not seek its own.* Grouping these four together provides little nuances of the main concept of being self-centered. But God's love is altogether different.

## LOVE DOES NOT PARADE ITSELF

Let's begin with the first attribute, *"Love does not parade itself."* The Greek word Paul used for *not parade itself* only occurs here in the entire New Testament. Basically it means to be a braggart. It's interesting that the Greek word has the root meaning to cross the line, to go farther, or to go over. Today we would say they are way over the top. It's like they've crossed the line to unreasonableness or inappropriateness. It has to do with making oneself appear larger than life.

Beware of the person who constantly talks about their own good deeds and accomplishments. They have to fit their deeds into every conversation they have. It's almost as if you hear them say, "Enough of me talking about me; now you talk about me for awhile."

God's love is not like this. A Bible commentary by William Barclay says, *"True love is always far more impressed with its own unworthiness than its own merit."*

After being a Christian for a while, we can tend to think we're so spiritual when we do something right. Yet we so easily forget what we were like when God first rescued us. It's one thing to be used by the Lord to do a good deed, but it's another thing to make sure everyone is convinced at how good we are. Jesus said to His disciples, "Let your light so shine before men that they may see your good works and glorify your Father who is in Heaven." The whole purpose is to glorify our heavenly Father, not to glorify us as the vessel.

When something good takes place and God uses us, our flesh is always right there to try to take the credit, the accolade, to put the garland around ourselves. Mortification is the only answer for our flesh as it seeks to get in there and rip off the glory. God will not share His glory with anyone.

**Isaiah 42:8** *I am the LORD, that is My name; And My glory I will not give to another, Nor My praise to carved images.*

If God uses us to accomplish something good in service to Him, it's to be for His glory 100 percent of the time. There'll be times when we'll faithfully do what is right and instead of favor from others, we receive persecution. We must understand that the reward for our faithfulness comes when we see Jesus. If God happens to bless our lives here on earth, we should count it as a special blessing, but it's not the reward.

How did *"love does not parade itself"* apply to the Corinthian believers? There were those among the believers in the church who were outwardly boasting of their spiritual gifts and their special advantages. Those whose personalities were very aggressive and controlling were yielding to the temptation to 'go way over the top' regarding the spiritual gifts God had given them. They were easily justifying their attitudes by saying, "I'm just giving God the glory" when in effect, it was all about how spiritual they thought themselves to be.

Satan seeks to lull us into the same trap that he himself fell into: becoming self-deceived, conceited and thinking more highly of ourselves than we ought to think. None of us can completely know our own heart. What we can do, though, is to ask God to search our hearts so we can have a clear conscience about it.

**Romans 12:3** *For I say, through the grace given to me, to everyone who is among you, not to think of himself more highly than he ought to think, but to think soberly, as God has dealt to each one a measure of faith.*

It's right for us to have a clear conscience before God. But still there's a lot of dross that must be dredged up and removed from our hearts. God deals with us in His grace. I'm so glad for this because none of us could stand the test of perfection if it was based on our good deeds.

## TROUBLE ON THE HOME FRONT

What does this aspect of God's love look like in action in our marriages? God's love doesn't express itself by pressing to take the credit when something works out in a marriage situation. I think it's under the title, 'I told you so.' It doesn't put us forward to prove how right and smart we were, and, in effect, implying how our spouse is so lame and clueless.

One sure way to kill affection in a marriage is to constantly boast about our good deeds to our spouse. If we did something to bless our spouse, and he or she doesn't recognize it, then let it go. Blessing another is to happen without expecting to be paid back. If we find there's resentment in us because they didn't acknowledge our good deed toward them, it shows that we were doing it to manipulate them in some way in the first place.

Sometimes we try to get fulfillment from our spouse when we should be getting it from God. Listen, a spouse is not always going to respond. They have bad days, too. There are times when they aren't very happy about us, either. We need to get our joy and fulfillment first from God and take the pressure off our spouses. Reminding a spouse of how smart we are, how good we are, and how wise we are is parading ourselves. We're doing what the Bible says God's love doesn't do.

How would this apply to us as parents? It's our responsibility as parents to help our children learn how to have a biblical view of their life. There's a lot of talk today about positive self-esteem. I understand the goal; it means to not be beaten down, to have confidence, assurance, security, order, purpose, and to know where you're going. However, the focus is self. Self becomes the standard. As a Christian, we know that there's a higher standard than self. God has called us to have a biblical view, which is a higher level than just a positive, healthy self-esteem. What is meant by a biblical view of life? The world system around us speaks much about good self-esteem, and how we should view ourselves in light of ourselves. But for the Christian, there's something better, something more accurate, and healthy. We view our lives as children of God in light of what He says about us in His word, and not by how the world views us.

When we're feeling bad about ourselves because of what has happened around us, we have to default back to this: what does God say about me and my situation? It's not about how I feel. Let His Word give us the biblical view of our lives. As parents, we need to first have that solidly in our own lives. If we don't have that right, how are we going to communicate it to our children? We need to see ourselves in His perfection, because the perfection of Jesus has been put to our account by the grace of God through faith in Jesus.

## STRIVING FOR EXCELLENCE
## TO GLORIFY GOD

It's right to strive for excellence in everything we do, whether it's in our secular job, our sporting events, or even our parenting. But for the Christian the goal is so different from the world system. Our goal isn't for the plaque, trophy, or getting first place.

For the Christian, there's another motive, a higher focus: to glorify God. The first answer of the Westminster confession to the question, 'what is the chief end of man' is this: "The chief end of man is to glorify God and to enjoy

Him forever." Glorifying God and enjoying Him is very essential to our whole purpose. What we do may not be up to the level of someone else's standard of excellence, but the One who judges us is God and not man. For the Christian, you have to take what God has put into your hand and do your best with it. Work with it as best as you can given your skill level and what you have to work with. The rest is up to God. I'm reminded of David, King of Israel. Whatever he did, he did with all his might and for a different purpose than to show off. He was doing what he did to glorify God, and he was doing it with all of his might.

For a Christian to walk in pride and arrogance, to become haughty and self-centered is not of God. It'll lead to being chastened by God. God loves those He chastens, but He does indeed chasten.

**Hebrews 12:5-6**
*⁵ And you have forgotten the exhortation which speaks to you as to sons: "My son, do not despise the chastening of the LORD, Nor be discouraged when you are rebuked by Him; ⁶ For whom the LORD loves He chastens, And scourges every son whom He receives."*

## LOVE IS NOT PUFFED UP

*Love is not puffed up.* There's a connection between 'does not parade itself' and 'is not puffed up.' *Does not parade itself* refers to the outward show that reflects the inward heart and attitude. Parading oneself addresses the outward expression, whereas puffed up addresses the inward attitude and mind set. Being puffed up has to do with becoming full of hot air, thinking of yourself more highly than you ought to think.

Puffed up simply means to inflate, to make proud, to be haughty in spirit, and to be inflated with one's own importance. In Robert's Word Pictures, he describes it as "puffing oneself out like a pair of bellows." Now let's see how this applies to the Corinthian believers. Seven times in the New Testament this Greek word for puffed up is used. Six of those seven applied to the Corinthian believers. Here are two of those places:

> **1 Corinthians 4:6** *Now these things, brethren, I have figuratively transferred to myself and Apollos for your sakes, that you may learn in us not to think beyond what is written, that none of you may be puffed up on behalf of one against the other.*

They were bragging about who had discipled them, and who had brought them to Christ. "I'm a disciple of Peter." "Well, I'm a disciple of Paul." "Hey, I was there with Jesus." They were trying to outdo the other person.

> **1 Corinthians 5:2** *And you are puffed up, and have not rather mourned, that he who has done this deed might be taken away from among you.*

The people in the church were thinking it was no big deal that one of their fellow believers was living in a sexual relationship with his stepmother. They were saying, "Oh, you know, we're tolerant these days; we understand that as long as they love each other—consenting adults and all." Paul tells them, "What? You have this arrogance and you think it doesn't matter that you go off into this kind of sin. Even the heathens don't do that these days. You're puffed up and have not rather mourned."

## MARRIAGES THAT MORPH

What does this puffed up attitude look like in a marriage? Think of when you first met your spouse. All of the sudden, there was this chemistry that started between you as a couple. Then you tended to look and smell your best around each other. You would think through the upcoming evening and make painstaking efforts to be sure everything was flawless. You presented yourselves in your best behavior. Oh, how you deferred to the other's interests and activities!

Then things progressed to the point of deciding to marry. Your proposal was hopefully well planned out and not merely a casual affair. Then there was the wedding itself and the sealing of the covenant for life. There may have been a few glitches in the overall event, but how glorious it was! The bride was more beautiful than you'd ever seen her. The groom was so handsome it made you proud to be his for life.

After the honeymoon, things can change ever so slightly. My plans, rights, goals, preferences, sense of duty, and feelings start to come to the forefront, and then the conflicts begin. You can almost hear the bellows start in the background puffing each of you up. What happened? What changed?

As believers, we can choose to walk in the Spirit of God every day, or we can choose to walk in selfishness and self-inflated opinions. It's a daily choice we must make. We have the Spirit of God living in us and have the ability to walk in the Spirit. We can't come to our spouse and say, "You know, I just couldn't help myself."

How is it that we who are indwelt by the Spirit of God can become so puffed up? It starts in little ways, with little subtle attitudes, little subtle mindsets that end up inflating our estimation of ourselves. At first, we don't see it. We start demanding that our needs be met first. If we don't deal with it in the beginning stages, then it subtly starts puffing us up.

The reality is we married a sinner who's being worked on by God just as we are. They don't always let the love of God control their life either. So the first thing we have to work on is ourselves. We must stop and humble ourselves before the Lord, admitting we're pushing our rights around. That's the first step in true repentance.

## FAMILIES AFFECTED BY SELFISHNESS

How do these truths apply to the family unit? As parents we need to be on the lookout for this puffed up attitude that occasionally appears in our children. Sometimes it'll show up in how they test us. There are days when from the moment they wake up and their feet touch the ground, it's all about them.

What we need to do is sit them down and tell them, "Look, you live in my world; I'm not living in yours. It's time right now to stop this attitude." We have to take control of the situation because we can't let that attitude rule them. They must learn how to deal with their bad days, and we're there to help them in that.

Sometimes our children may say, "I don't like you" or "I hate you" after they're corrected. It's their little effort to make us feel bad. What they're really doing is testing us. They don't know what else to say; they're children.

I would suggest having a family meeting on Sunday nights. Gather everyone together and say, "Look, here's how it works. I'm the Daddy and that's enough. She's the Mommy, and that's enough; we love you, but you've got to listen." We have to take control and bring in some sense of gravity into the home. Affirm your love toward them, but hold to the boundaries.

## LOVE DOES NOT BEHAVE RUDELY

Let's take a look at the third of these four pictures of self-centeredness: *love does not behave rudely*. It's interesting to me why Paul took the time to use these separate attributes. I believe it was because there were certain aspects of this whole self-centeredness issue that he wanted to point out.

When we examine various cultures in the world, rudeness is defined in different ways. It's rude in some countries to put our Bible on the floor. They believe it's dishonorable to God. In some cultures it's rude for a man to not take off his hat when he prays. To some people, using humor in a sermon is rude. To others, unless one is dressed in a shirt, tie, and a suit they aren't honoring God. But it's a cultural judgment call, and it changes depending on where we are.

So how should we define rudeness? We have to go back to Scripture and not to culture. The core meaning of the word rude has to do with that which is unrestrained, indecent, and ungracious; that which lacks courtesy, tact, and politeness.

When a believer uses the Word of God in a blunt and brutal way, it may have truth to it, but it lacks love, and that absolutely lessens the effectiveness of the truth. One translation puts it 'love is not ostentatious'. Although rudeness is a word which has varied meanings, it centers on the idea of vulgarity and loudness to attract attention.

When there's a filthiness, a vulgarity, an in-your-face kind of an attitude, it's rude. Some people believe that the end justifies the means. For them it's okay to use rudeness and threats to bring about a desired end. As long as it's a good end (at least in their minds), it doesn't matter how they accomplish it.

I've even personally watched it happen with Christian leaders seeking to get something at a bargain price. The rudeness by which they belittle the manager and seek to manipulate the transaction is a blot on the Christian testimony. "Oh, but I'm saving the Lord's money," they may say.

Listen, does saving the Lord's money give anyone a green light to be rude to people and blow the witness of Christ's love? No way! That behavior comes from the world's philosophy that the end justifies the means. When we yield to this we quench the flow of God's love from our life.

How did *love does not behave rudely* apply to the Corinthian believers? In 1 Corinthians 6, we find there were some in the church who were suing one another before the Roman courts. Those lawsuits were being filed against fellow Christians for the purpose of retribution. There was no attempt at reconciliation by consulting the church leaders or attempting to walk in God's love.

There were others in the church who despised fellow believers who had problems eating food that had been offered to idols; they were despising them and thinking, "Why don't you guys grow up? It's just food." But others who had been involved with idolatry knew exactly what was going on with this food. They couldn't in clear conscience partake. They ended up judging those who had the supposed liberty.

There were those who were drinking the communion wine at the Lord's Table and getting drunk, as well as eating the majority of the food at the fellowship dinner, leaving little for the rest of the group. Talk about rudeness. Did they deserve Paul's rebuke? Absolutely!

## RUDENESS RUINS RELATIONSHIPS

How do these things apply to our marriages today? Have we been rude to our spouse in the name of rightness, in the name of it's-not-fair, in the name of trying to get them to go along with us? So we're rude and beat them down, belittle them, swear at them, use vulgarity and verbal abuse against them to accomplish our ends.

First of all, that's not only rudeness but sin as well. Each word, each phrase is building a wall, brick by brick, between our spouse and us. Rudeness will kill affection. The problem with rudeness is that it blinds us from seeing we're the one building the wall and then we blame them for being so distant.

In families, honor and respect are to be the major goals. Rudeness between siblings will destroy that respect, and become a constant fight. We need a family meeting to get this identified. Honor and respect have to be more important than anything else in our families. Our children must respect each other. Having them work things out if they have offended the other is so important.

## LOVE DOES NOT SEEK ITS OWN

The fourth attribute of God's love is *Love does not seek its own*. This is more of a general term. The Greek word used for seek its own means 'to insist upon one's own way, one's own rights, and one's own interests.'

William Barclay, the Bible commentator says, "There are in this world only two kinds of people, those who always insist upon their privileges and those who always remember their responsibilities. Those who are always thinking of what life owes them and those who never forget what they owe to life. It would be the key to almost all the problems which surround us today if men would think less of their rights and more of their duties. Whenever we start thinking about our place, we're drifting away from Christian love."

So, how did this attribute apply to the Corinthian believers? It was addressing their overall problem which had subtly crept into the church, probably after Paul left. Paul had spent a year and a half discipling them. Then he had to leave and go to other countries, and it appears like they started quickly to develop factions among themselves. Selfishness and self-centeredness was at the core of all of it.

There was this attitude among them that started to run rampant in their midst, an attitude that implied, "My interests are the most important thing to be considered by others"; and it led to divisions, suspicions, jealousies, and to unfounded accusations. What kind of witness was being given to the rest of the town of Corinth?

The Corinthians weren't powerless to change. They had the ability to stop and turn things around. But people don't turn around from a behavior they're committing until they understand the damage they're doing to others and to themselves. Selfishness can so captivate the human mind. It's all so justified, so right at first, but it destroys. It doesn't build up.

So how does 'love does not seek its own' show itself in the marriage relationship? Our spouses don't think about us all the time. Do we think about our spouses 24/7? Maybe the real motive is that we think about them in light of how they can benefit us. But then, it's really all about us. We need to take that pressure off our spouse.

Here's an assignment for us as married couples. In the next forty-eight hours, let's ask the Lord to show us how to bless our spouse in ways that connect with them. Let it be unilateral, one way, like shooting a light beam into space. Let's willingly set aside the differences that may have separated us in the past.

Now, let's expand this assignment further and apply it with our children. Let's take them individually and go over to a mall or some other store, maybe even simply to get an ice cream cone and be with them. If we'd bless them in their little world, we might be surprised at what comes out of their hearts and mouths. All of the sudden, they aren't fighting for our attention. But we need to take that time separately with them; it's part of loving them with God's love.

It's important that these four descriptions of what God's love is not like be removed from our witness as Christians. Let's ask the Lord to show us if there are areas where we're allowing these things to have a foothold and we may be turning a blind eye to them.

# CHAPTER 7

## ⁓ LOVE DOES NOT HAVE ⁓ A SHORT FUSE

I was raised in a Christian home. My dad and mom were church going people, but we had family difficulties. My mother had grand mal epilepsy, so she could never hold down a job nor drive a car. The seizures were so sudden and severe that she didn't even have time to protect herself. My dad was a school administrator and tried to do the best he could on that small salary. My sister was five years older than me, so I was left alone with my mom as a preschooler. The seizures occurred every week or two, even though she was on medication. When she would go into a seizure, it was my responsibility to come to where she was and try to lay her down so she wouldn't fall on something and hurt herself.

My dad was good at trying to explain it all to me, but as a little child, it was still pretty traumatic. It would also happen sometimes in front of my friends who were over at the house. At that age, I didn't know how to process it. I wanted her to stop. I'd yell at her to stop and I would hit her. "Stop, please stop this," I'd shout. This built up an angry habit within me over those early years. Whenever I'd encounter life situations that were frustrating or when I didn't get my way, I'd go into these angry tirades.

My dad was the principal at the local grade school. I remember when I began first grade. I'd learned over time that the way to deal with frustration was to swing it out. There was this one kid, Steven, who'd make me so mad each morning during recess before class. I'd inevitably end up fighting him.

Little Bobby at age 3

Alta, Beverly, Elmer, and Bobby age 4

So here were these two little first graders flailing at each other and, of course, we'd get hauled into my dad's office because he was the principal. We both got the 'board of education,' one swift swat on the behind, and then I also got reprimanded later at home. I know that in my flesh things got patterned because of what I had to deal with regularly. As I grew into my teen years that anger turned into a rebellious attitude. When I was a sophomore in High School my mother died of cancer. Because I'd built up a wall in my own emotions against her, at first I was unfazed by her passing. But then, in what I believe was an unconscious way to deal with my guilt and the loss of closeness with my mom, I began to experiment with recreational drugs. I also pulled away from my church background and explored various Eastern religions, spiritism, and the occult. I poured myself into the rock band I was in as we traveled all over the Northwestern part of the country.

As I mentioned earlier in this book, it was at age eighteen that I surrendered my life to Jesus Christ. My girlfriend also accepted Christ at that time. We were married six months later. There was a lot of heart-washing, a lot of crying that went on within me. The Lord began to deal with me in this area of my angry spirit. When frustration would come about in our marriage, I remember not knowing what to do. The Lord has ways of breaking us and showing us that there's a better way to deal with these issues. His love begins the process of healing, restoring, and educating.

## THE SHORT FUSE EXCUSE

It's interesting to find that so many people have deeply ingrained anger issues. I believe much of the time those patterns of anger are formed long before we grow into adulthood. Sometimes we can think that we're the only one who has to deal with it.

I've had the privilege of traveling to many different countries over the years. Generally those journeys were centered around short-term mission projects, either leading small teams or being a member of one. Invariably, I'd come across a person from that culture who'd make the statement that their people were the hot-headed and short-tempered ones. But then how is it that every ethnic group thinks they have a corner on having a short fuse?

As Christians, we can't excuse short-temperedness on our ethnic origin. Those outbursts come right out of our own sin nature, not from God's Spirit. This is what the apostle Paul was seeking to show in 1 Corinthians 13.

God's love *is not provoked.* Just what does that mean? When you look at all the attributes of God's love, it's interesting that the apostle Paul put *love is not provoked* right after the four descriptions of self-centeredness: *love does not parade itself, is not puffed up, does not behave rudely and does not seek its own.* When someone treats us in these ways, it can push our buttons. It can bring out the worst in us and provoke us to be a less than likable person.

In the midst of his multi-faceted description of God's love, Paul included this separate expression of *is not provoked.* The Greek word used means 'to exasperate, to have irritation or sharpness of spirit, to be provoked.' Other translations use "touchy or fretful or resentful" (AMP); "to blaze out in passionate anger" (Weymouth-NT in Modem Speech). God's love is not like that.

William Barclay writes in his *Daily Study Bible*: *"Love never flies into a temper. The real meaning of this is that Christian love never becomes exasperated with people. Exasperation is always a sign of defeat. When we lose our tempers, we lose everything."*

Even worldly philosophers recognize the value of having control over our own human spirit. Rudyard Kipling wrote:

*"If you can keep your head when all about you are losing theirs and blaming it on you; If you can trust yourself when all men doubt you, but make allowance for their doubting too; If you can meet with Triumph and Disaster and treat those two impostors just the same; Yours is the Earth and everything that's in it."*

A person can have a measure of control over their own human spirit by the power of their will. They see the repercussions of giving place to their anger, and they don't want to go there. They can have it all refined for the rest of their life.

But God has a much higher goal for us. He wants to work in us so we can reflect what He's like to this world. He starts changing our inner character; and if we have a real issue with anger, God wants to work right there. He doesn't throw us off saying, "You're just an angry kid; I want you out of My house."

He looks at us in His love and says, "I can heal what's going on in you because I know why you're the way you are, and I know how to fix it." Much of His work in us is to get us to believe Him and to know that He cares and can do what He's promised to do.

We fight against that and have this philosophy: "That's just the way I've always been. Look, if you cross me, you'll wish you never even met me in the first place." "Might is right" according to our thinking. We don't realize that when we act that way we're the lonesome victor. In that case we may think we've won, but we've lost. Everybody's gone, and we're by ourselves because we've driven them all away.

## IN OTHER WORDS...

There are quite a few synonyms that go along with this word *provoked*. A thesaurus can give a treasure trove of words and terms: *being in a fit of rage, fury, fit of pique, tantrum, bad mood, sulk, huff, grump, snit, hissy fit, fly into a rage, erupt, lose control, go berserk, breathe fire, flare up, boil over, go mad, go crazy, go bananas, have a fit, see red, fly off the handle, blow one's top, hit the roof, go off the deep end, go ape, flip out and freak out.*

Now if these terms describe our behavior, we have to conclude that God's love doesn't exhibit itself through us in those ways. We're not glorifying the Lord by letting loose those kinds of tirades.

We all have our angry moments, we've all sinned in this way, and some of us more than others. Sometimes the damage has long-lasting results, though. Anger management classes can help a little, but what is needed is to have real brokenness and humility in our spirit before God. The Holy Spirit of God can change an angry person into a loving person.

God's love isn't provoked and it doesn't fly off the handle. Over the more than forty three years of being a Christian, God has done a great work in me. The problem is, I still live in this body. I still have to put a guard on that gate of my life. That fingerprint of sinful anger still has left its mark. I have to make a choice, a step of faith, to direct my spirit into God's love by the Holy Spirit when I get frustrated or upset.

As Christians we're not allowed to fly off the handle, blow our top, hit the roof, go off the deep end, go ape, flip out, or freak out. God is in the process of healing every area of our lives. This is one area that sometimes is the dirty little secret in a marriage. The anger, the fists through the wall, the slamming of the doors—that's an attempt to control, to get our way.

Anger so often is simply the result of selfishness in our lives. We don't get our way, and we want to be in control. We're feeling out of control and in chaos inwardly, so we're trying to control our outward world. The answer is to humble ourselves before God and stop trying to control our world. He can turn us into a loving person.

Look at the apostle Paul before he was converted to Christianity. He'd used those heretics that were called Christians to be the target of his frustration, anger, and self righteousness. But God softened his heart and changed him. He had to go through temporary blindness to be humbled, though. Paul used this term *is not provoked* with the Corinthian believers because so many of them were not walking in God's love. They were being divisive and were taking each other before Roman courts. They were boasting about which spiritual gift they'd been given. There was so much provoking going on.

The Corinthian believers needed God's love more than they needed spiritual gifts, more than they needed super mentors. They needed God's love, which is why I believe Paul included that in this list. Sowing to the flesh in anger brings out the worst in you and in others. It's so easy to push someone else's buttons and then blame them for crossing the line.

## SETTING BOUNDARIES ON ANGER

So what does God want to do in us in this area? How does He want to do it? Let's take a look at some Scriptures on how to let go of anger. It's obvious that even in the Old Testament times a person had the ability to put boundaries over their angry behavior. They didn't have the indwelling Holy Spirit under the old covenant, but they did have God's law that gave them boundaries and structure.

**Psalm 4:4-5**
*[4] Be angry, and do not sin. Meditate within your heart on your bed, and be still. Selah [5] Offer the sacrifices of righteousness And put your trust in the LORD.*

These verses talk about letting go unto the Lord. There are things that should make us angry; injustices and true evil. Anger is a right response to true evil, but it's what we do with anger that matters. When anger rises up, we're at a crossroad; and unless we direct it into something constructive, Satan will be there to lead us down the path of destruction. Then he'll try to make us feel self-righteous over what we're angry about. When we express righteous anger in the wrong way, we become as guilty as the evil that stirred our heart in the first place.

So when anger comes up, we're not to let it turn into sinful anger. Meditate within our hearts on our beds; that means don't immediately react. We need to do something more than counting to ten. Ten is too quick. We have to stop and go over the situation as God would see it. Meditate within our hearts on our beds and be still.

The next verse says to offer the sacrifices of righteousness, which means doing what is right in the sight of the Lord according to His Word. It's a sacrifice because our flesh doesn't feel like doing anything else but being angry. When we're angry, our passions are stirred, our emotions are stirred, our nostrils are flared, and our adrenaline is going. But a sacrifice is a sacrifice, and we have to settle down and walk in the fear of the Lord. Doing what's right means we take the whole matter and trust the Lord with it.

**Proverbs 14:29** *He who is slow to wrath has great understanding, But he who is impulsive exalts folly.*

We can know these things in our minds but when someone ticks us off, all of the sudden, we shift from 110 volts to 220 volts. The agitated emotions overwhelm wisdom, and that's right where we have to ask the Lord to intervene. As Christians we're to reflect the love of God and not the anger of man.

The power to live a life free from anger was difficult to find under the old covenant because one always had to be exhorted from the outside. The new covenant brings the law of God right into our hearts. The Holy Spirit comes in and He's not only our Counselor, He's our *dunamis*: our dynamite, power, and our ability to carry out what God says. That's such a tremendous hope. There are still choices we have to make. God will provide the counsel and the power, but we have to step out in faith to start the flow.

**Ephesians 4:31-32**
*[31] Let all bitterness, wrath, anger, clamor, and evil speaking be put away from you, with all malice. [32] And be kind to one another, tenderhearted, forgiving one another, even as God in Christ forgave you.*

Paul was writing to believers in the city of Ephesus. The exhortation was to resist yielding to bitterness, wrath, anger, clamor, and evil speaking. They were to be kind to one another, tenderhearted, forgiving one another, even as God in Christ had forgiven them.

It's possible as a Christian to be locked away in bitterness and unforgiveness against a person or even a group of people that have hurt us deeply. But to remain in that state isn't going to bring the needed healing in our lives. Rather, that soul damage will grow deeper and deeper. It's been said, living in bitterness and unforgiveness toward one who's offended us is like drinking poison and expecting the other person to die.

**James 1:19-20**
*[19] So then, my beloved brethren, let every man be swift to hear, slow to speak, slow to wrath; [20] for the wrath of man does not produce the righteousness of God.*

God is ready to work in our lives. These words aren't philosophies of famous men; these are the words of truth. And the Holy Spirit, who is called the Spirit of Truth, is ready to work in each and every one us right now to make this a reality. But we have to humble ourselves before the Lord and admit our weaknesses, failures, and inabilities to Him to make it happen.

## WHAT ANGER DOES TO RELATIONSHIPS

How do these truths apply to a couple who are thinking of getting married? When a couple first meets they say, "This is the best person I've ever met. Wow, I can't believe it." You're sort of in love with love at the beginning.

Then one offends the other and does something very selfish. Offenses are going to occur, but walking in God's love means that when we realize our friend has something against us, we ask their forgiveness for it and we own up to our sin. We take ownership of our wrongdoing because the relationship is more important than us being right.

We can't control what they're going to do. But by going to them and asking forgiveness, we're starting the process of healing and reconciliation. Sometimes the offense will be so bad we may never be best friends ever again. That's the reality of human relationships.

Sometimes we can bring a hyper-sensitivity into our anger issues. We're touchy and offended so easily the situation in which it occurred doesn't even matter. No one can make us happy; no one can please us because we have these open wounds. When anybody brushes against us, it's like all our nerve endings are agitated. No one can get close to us because as soon as they do, we feel hurt and see it as always their fault and ourselves as the victim. God wants to heal those wounds in our lives.

We'll never get close to anybody ever again if that mind set starts to rule and control our lives. *God's love is not provoked.* If we've had abuse in our family and in our life, Jehovah-Rapha, the Lord my Healer, wants to heal those hurts and teach us how to have holy love all over again. He can do that. It's going to be a fight, it's going to be hard, but it's not impossible because God's love is a healing love.

What does God's love look like in action in families where there has been constant fighting among the siblings? Maybe our brother or sister was the one who was always favored by dad and we were the one that didn't quite make the grade in his eyes. Now anything that comes close to that kind of circumstance sets us off. God wants to change that in our hearts. Dad probably had his issues as well. He may have been dealing with us through his own issues and wasn't handling things correctly.

God wants to heal our lives so we can love our brother or sister with a true love. It doesn't start with behavior modification. It starts with brokenness, the power of the Holy Spirit, and seeing God's love for what it is and what He's done for us.

Maybe we have a real bitterness and resentment against our mother or father for what happened when we were growing up, and it's caused us to be touchy, to take everything as a personal offense.

We have to see it for what it is and say, "God, I don't want to live my life like this. I'm trapped. I want You to heal me." He can do it, but it's going to be hard and painful at times, because there's no other way through it. We have to face things, but Jesus is right there with us, He has His arm around us saying, "Hey, we can do this; it's all right, and I'm in this with you for the long haul."

Since God's love is not provoked, the movement of the Holy Spirit will be to carry us stage by stage to live in the freedom of His grace and love.

# CHAPTER 8

## LOVE KEEPS NO RECORD OF WRONGS SUFFERED

It was one of the most difficult years for our family. Finances were scarce no matter how hard we tried to make ends meet. Each month was an adventure on how to juggle the grace periods from all the bills and keep from having our utilities shut off.

My wife and I were working as much as we could, but the level of our hourly wages was meager. The children weren't aware of how serious things had become.

It was at that time when we received a call from an acquaintance asking if we'd be interested in taking over their evening office cleaning responsibilities for a few weeks. They'd send the money to us when their client paid them for that time. It was an answer to prayer... or so we thought.

After the orientation, we packed our three children in the car and headed out to the office complex. I strapped our youngest son into the baby carrier on my back and the two older boys helped with emptying the trash cans. Although it was tiring the children didn't complain too much and we accomplished the task.

We waited and waited for our friend to send us the check. After six weeks I called him and asked him about it. He said they had not sent it to him yet. We waited another couple of weeks and still no money arrived. I called again and he said there was some mix up at the client's office and the check was forthcoming.

Three months later I called and demanded to know what was going on. It was then he confessed to me he'd spent the money because of his own family's needs and was afraid to tell me. He apologized, asked my forgiveness, and then said he wasn't going to be able to pay us.

At first, I wanted to reach through that phone line and get a hold of the guy's throat. After all, MY family had great needs, too. How could he, a Christian brother, a fellow church member, do this to another one of God's children? And then the lying, deceitfulness, and sheer boldness to make up stories to me week after week.

It was right at that moment when the Holy Spirit nudged my spirit and brought to mind the words of the Lord Jesus in His model prayer, "Forgive us our trespasses as we forgive those who trespass against us." I was to release this brother and forgive his debt against my family. God would provide all that we would need day by day.

I said to him on the phone, "Brother, I completely release you from this debt. Our fellowship together is more important than a few bucks. God will take care of the needs of both our families."

At first I was shocked I actually said that. My flesh was rising up and saying, "No, No, No! Don't let the guy get away with it." But the inner witness of the Holy Spirit continually confirmed that what I'd done was the right thing, at the right time, in the right way.

As I look back on that incident, I can see how God was using it to shape my character to be conformed into the image of His Son. His love thinks no evil, and keeps no record of wrongs suffered.

## SHREDDING THE EVIDENCE

The next attribute of God's love mentioned in the last part of 1 Corinthians verse 5 is *love thinks no evil*. Unfortunately, the English translation doesn't give us the fullest meaning of the Greek word Paul used here for *thinks*. The word *think* has to do with 'taking an account of, keeping a record of, a regular going over the list of the offenses someone has committed against us'. Thinks no evil then has to do with focusing on the offense and thinking about it all the time, instead of letting it go and giving it to God.

Here are a couple of translations that put this into perspective. The Amplified Bible says, *Love takes no account of the evil done to it [it pays no attention to a suffered wrong].* The New Living translation reads, *Love keeps no record of being wronged.*

Thinks no evil has to do with mulling over the wrongs people have committed against us—over and over and over again. If God's love keeps no record of being wronged, then when we live and abide in God's love, we're not going to be mulling over what wrongs others have done to us. It's not a quality of God's love.

God doesn't keep a record of our wrongs. He doesn't look at our life and say, "Do you know how many times you've done that? Do you know how many times you've failed Me?" Do you think God goes over all the wrongs we've done against Him over and over again? Do you think He mulls and stews over it, and gets hot under the collar?

The Bible doesn't portray God's love in that way. His love thinks no evil, even though we've surely offended God many times. God's love doesn't keep a record of wrongs. What if He held us to the same standards that we may be holding others to who have wronged us? This isn't how God sees us in Christ.

How is this possible with Him? It's because of His love. The price for our wrongs against Him has been paid. Justice has been served. It's not amnesty; it's a payment. Justice demands payment, and that's what Jesus came to do: He made the payment for our sins against Him. Justice has been served through the death of Christ.

Somebody might say, "What if a person commits a criminal act against me and harms my family? Are you saying I just have to forget all that?" No, that's not what is being said here. If we've been eaten up by the evil that's happened to us, that's something God wants to heal in us.

## EVIL HAPPENS

This life is full of selfishness, evil, sin, and criminal activity. Sometimes things have happened to us that weren't fair. In fact they were downright evil. But we can so focus on the wrongs others have committed against us that it completely eats up our life. It affects how we deal with everybody else because we're hanging onto it. Yet God's love takes no account of the evil done.

One reason we hold on to the offenses of others against us is our own fear. We're afraid if we don't hold on to it, no one else will, and then the person will go free. God wants us to deal with evil that comes to us; not by ignoring it, denying it, and not by pretending it never happened. He doesn't want us to let it consume our life. God desires we come to the place where we give it to Jesus. Those very wrongs that have been done to us or to those we love have been borne by the Lord Jesus on the cross.

Knowing that is one thing, actually living it out is an entirely different matter. It's going to take the power and healing of God to bring us to that place of letting go. Evil is evil. It's right to be grieved over a crime that's happened to us. There'll be pain over the offense. Maybe our entire childhood was ruined, or our marriage collapsed, and it destroyed our life.

Evil happened; but what are we going to do with it? Are we going to let it consume us? If we do that we'll be eaten up from the inside out. This isn't God's plan for us. When God rescued us from the 'world's orphanage', He brought us into His own life, heart, and family. He put His spirit right within us. His design was to set us free on the inside. His desire was for us was to go forward in His love and He'd bring the healing to our soul. Sure, there's emotional healing that needs to take place, but Psalm 23 tells us when the Lord is our Shepherd, He restores our soul.

We have an overriding, tremendous hope, no matter what's happened to us. We have this hope because God will take all things, and work something good out of them according to His purpose. Without that reality, there's no real hope concerning all the evil that's going on in the world.

God is faithful. He makes promises that are true, and He loves us unconditionally. God wants to bless our lives each day, even in this area of healing. But we have to open our arms to Him and take a risk; let go of the wrongs others have committed against us. We're to release them into the hands of the Judge of all things. Know that it'll be taken care of in heaven's court.

There's a connection, I believe, between us letting go, and us experiencing a fullness of God's grace within our lives. Jesus said this to His disciples in Matthew 6:

**Matthew 6:14-15**
*14 For if you forgive men their trespasses, your heavenly Father will also forgive you. 15 But if you do not forgive men their trespasses, neither will your Father forgive your trespasses.*

It's easy for us to say we believe that; but at times, it seems impossible to carry out except for the grace of God. God's love keeps no record of wrongs suffered.

Here's a suggestion: let's take a couple of sheets of paper and write on them all the wrongs we can think of that people have committed against us. Get it all out, write it all down. Then we lay our hand on those papers and say, "God, You know these things very well. Your Word says that all these offenses were borne by my Lord Jesus, along with my own sins. So, by a step of faith, I want to commit these to You and let go."

Then we take our list over to the shredder, put it in, and don't look back. Of course, our minds might want to go back and think about those evils, but we're to erase them from our minds because we've already taken that step of faith. The Holy Spirit wants to do a cleansing and washing in our lives, but there are initial steps of faith we need to take, because that's what is required. Without faith, it's impossible to please God.

## GUARDING YOUR THOUGHT LIFE

Our thought life is a key element in our Christian walk. We can choose to spend time focusing on all the wrongs people have done to us, or we can spend time focusing on all the blessings God has given to us. There's a connection God has made between our thought life and our emotional life. I'm not talking about the power of positive thinking here.

God has given us so many things to ponder concerning what He's done for us. We can think of all He has for us in the future, not just what He's done for us in the past, and how He's with us right now in the present. We have this future, this inheritance, of being with Him forever that makes the wrongs which have happened to us diminish.

Reading through Psalm 103, we're brought face to face with so many things the Lord has promised to do in our lives. Here are just a few in the first verses of that psalm:

**Psalm 103:1-5**
*¹ Bless the LORD, O my soul; And all that is within me, bless His holy name! ² Bless the LORD, O my soul, And forget not all His benefits: ³ Who forgives*

*all your iniquities, Who heals all your diseases, <sup>4</sup>*
*Who redeems your life from destruction, Who crowns*
*you with lovingkindness and tender mercies, <sup>5</sup> Who*
*satisfies your mouth with good things, So that your*
*youth is renewed like the eagle's.*

God has indeed done so many things for us. We don't
even touch the amount of time we should spend thanking
Him for all He's done. We don't know how many ways He's
protected us already. We don't realize how many angels
were involved with our protection today. We'll not see it until
we get to heaven; but yet, in spite of all these benefits, we
can spend our time focusing on the wrongs others have done
against us.

As I mentioned in the previous chapter, having bitterness
and unforgiveness against someone who has wronged us is
like drinking poison and expecting them to die. We're the
ones who suffer. Where is the freedom? It'll only come by
the power of God when we step out in faith and release those
who have wronged us.

**Romans 8:28** *And we know that all things work*
*together for good to those who love God, to those*
*who are the called according to His purpose.*

It may take some time for the Holy Spirit to bring us
to the place of courage where we can let go, in spite of all
that's happened to us. When we look at the things Paul wrote
in 1 Corinthians 13, remember that he had the Corinthian
church in mind. Right after he said love *is not provoked*, he
adds love *thinks no evil*, which means love keeps no record
of wrongs.

I believe there's a purposed connection between the two
expressions. When we have a short fuse, we tend to build a
record of wrongs in our minds. So the very next point Paul

makes is, "By the way, love doesn't write down and keep mulling over the record of wrongs that's been committed against you." There were some strong believers in the church in Corinth, but many struggled with carnality in their daily behavior and attitude. They were defrauding one another, ripping each other off, and generally not walking in God's love toward one another. They were saying, "We have all this special knowledge and all these Spiritual gifts," but they weren't walking in God's love. Let's take a look at these two Old Testament Scriptures.

**Proverb 10:12** *Hatred stirs up strife, But love covers all sin.*

When our heart is locked up by hatred, and we're not letting go of those offenses, it'll stir up strife in us wherever we go. In every situation, it'll find a cause and then express itself. But true love covers all sins.

**Proverb 17:9** *He who covers a transgression seeks love, But he who repeats a matter separates friends.*

This Scripture is frequently mentioned when I officiate at weddings because a husband and wife are going to offend one another on a fairly regular basis as the years go by. If we keep bringing up matters that have been supposedly resolved, forgiveness asked for and granted, it's a guarantee that we'll kill affection in our marriage. Why? Anyone who repeats a matter (a transgression) will separate friends. The affection, friendship, and the fondness of love will start dying out.

## LOVING YOUR ENEMIES

Let's look at the New Testament, starting with a quote from Jesus in Matthew 5:

**Matthew 5:44-45**
*44 But I say to you, love your enemies, bless those who curse you, do good to those who hate you, and pray for those who spitefully use you and persecute you, 45 that you may be sons of your Father in heaven; for He makes His sun rise on the evil and on the good, and sends rain on the just and on the unjust.*

It's not natural for us to do this, to love our enemies, to bless those who curse us, and to do good to those who hate us. We usually prefer people to like us, and we have to be careful that we don't become a man pleaser. It's an awful feeling to have somebody hate us, especially when we've tried to make reconciliation, and they still hate us.

So what are we supposed to do? Should we say, "Well, if they're going to hate me, then I'll hate them"? This kind of attitude will cause us to become trapped and will destroy us on the inside.

What does Jesus say to do when we have enemies? What does He say to do when people curse at us, when people hate us, and when people abuse and use us? The counsel from Jesus is: love them, bless them, do good to them, and pray for them.

When we step out in faith in these areas (not because we feel like it, but because we want to obey what the Lord instructs us to do) the Holy Spirit is right there to begin His work in our heart. We might say, "Yeah, I'm praying for them but they're not changing." The most important work in this entire process is what goes on in our heart, not what we want to see in their life. God is going to allow His love to start flowing through us again. In Colossians 3:13-14 Paul is writing to Christians in the church at Colossae.

**Colossians 3:13-14**
*[13] bearing with one another, and forgiving one another, if anyone has a complaint against another; even as Christ forgave you, so you also must do. [14] But above all these things put on love, which is the bond of perfection.*

Take a look at what the apostle Peter says in 1 Peter 2:20-25.

**1 Peter 2:20-25**
*[20] For what credit is it if, when you are beaten for your faults, you take it patiently? But when you do good and suffer, if you take it patiently, this is commendable before God. [21] For to this you were called, because Christ also suffered for us, leaving us an example, that you should follow His steps: [22] "Who committed no sin, Nor was deceit found in His mouth"; [23] who, when He was reviled, did not revile in return; when He suffered, He did not threaten, but committed Himself to Him who judges righteously; [24] who Himself bore our sins in His own body on the tree, that we, having died to sins, might live for righteousness—by whose stripes you were healed. [25] For you were like sheep going astray, but have now returned to the Shepherd and Overseer of your souls.*

After reading these Scriptures we might be thinking, "I can't do this. I just can't carry out what it says." But the Spirit of God in us can start doing that work to nudge us and push us into this area of obedience so we can experience the blessing that's behind His counsel. There's this battle between the flesh and the Spirit. We should say, "You know what? I have to try; I have to step out in faith."

## LETTING GO OF PAST OFFENSES TOWARD OTHERS

Let's consider how these Scriptures apply to marriage. Picture two people standing at the altar ready to make their wedding vows. They've committed to come into a covenant before God to be faithful to one another, to love and cherish one another until death parts them. At that time, there's no thought of divorce nor of leaving or abandoning the other person. They're in love, it's an exciting time.

But how does it all unravel? The relationship begins to fragment when they start keeping a record of wrongs against each other. Our spouse is going to offend us at some point. They're going to do something wrong that upsets us. When that starts happening and the emotions start rising up, then we can find ourselves saying, "Well, you know what? Unless they come to me, then I'm just going to give them the silent treatment. That'll show them I'm really upset."

That'll easily lead to our spouse thinking, "Really! Is this the way it's going to be? Well, we'll just see how long this lasts." Pretty soon, the home is quieter than it's ever been in a long time. Affection is quickly dying out because all the while we're keeping silent and playing this little game. We're constantly thinking about the wrongs of our spouse. But it's affecting our life, it's affecting our emotions and affection is dying out. That's why the Scripture says if you're angry, sin not. Don't let the sun go down on your wrath.

We can't force a peace to take place that night between our spouse and us. We can't say, "We're staying up until this gets resolved. I don't care if I never get any sleep."

In marriage, we need to be the first to repent. We need to be the first to let it go, to be the first to take the wrongs committed against us, and set them before the Judge of all. Then love our spouse instead of returning the wrong.

How does this work in family life? God has called us as parents to forgive our children, our parents, and our grandparents. Unless we let go of those wrongs, it'll affect our future relationships. It'll subtly create a hyper-sensitive mind set where everything that happens to us is viewed in the light of us always being the victim. It'll begin to destroy us from the inside out.

Maybe a girlfriend or boyfriend had our hopes up, and we're thinking it was going to lead to engagement, then marriage. Suddenly, we discovered they went out with someone else without our knowledge. Not only that, they were intimate with them.

Now we're thinking, "You know what? I'm blocking that person out of my life; I'm not going to let myself get near anyone anymore." Listen, we have to let go of that because we'll never move forward in our future relationships with others until we've been released from it.

Sure, this is easy to talk about, but gut wrenching to go through. God is faithful, though, to help us; and God is powerful enough to heal our hearts. The best news is this: God is waiting to do these things in us right now. Let's take a step of faith upon the promises of God in this area of our lives. He'll surprise us with His grace.

# CHAPTER 9

## ∼ℚ LOVE REJOICES IN ℚ∼ THE TRUTH

There had been such a radical change in my heart that took place after I trusted Christ for my salvation. My life had been full of immorality, in thought, words, and deeds. It was nothing to laugh and gloat over things that now I consider unspeakable. My music reflected this, my poetry reflected this, and my goals reflected this.

But when I surrendered my life to Christ there was a washing that began within me. Little by little those same immoral things I rejoiced in previously, became grieving to my spirit. I remember taking all my occult books and record albums and burning them in the fifty gallon barrel in the backyard. Although I'd spent hundreds of dollars over the years purchasing those items, I now wanted a clean slate. I wanted nothing surrounding my life that could be used to pull me back into that realm of unholiness.

This touches upon what will be covered in this chapter: Love Rejoices in the Truth. As a believer in Christ Jesus who is filled with God's love, there should be a move away from unholy living. There should be a new longing toward purity and holiness in the things that are right and true.

### INIQUITY, TRANSGRESSION, AND SIN

First Corinthians 13:6 says, *[Love] does not rejoice in iniquity, but rejoices in the truth.* When we examine the word *iniquity* in Scripture, we'll find other words linked with it— transgression, and sin. It's very important that we understand the difference between these words. As we look through Scripture, sometimes these words seem interchangeable. The context of the verse determines the particular definition. Do you remember reading in the book of Exodus when Moses was up on Mount Sinai? He wanted to see God's glory, so God hid him in a cleft of a rock. Then He put His hand over Moses and went by him, proclaiming the name of the Lord. The Lord's name was His character, His very nature.

**Exodus 34:6-7**
*6 And the LORD passed before him and proclaimed, 'The LORD, the LORD God, merciful and gracious, longsuffering, and abounding in goodness and truth, 7 keeping mercy for thousands, forgiving iniquity and transgression and sin, by no means clearing the guilty, visiting the iniquity of the fathers upon the children and the children's children to the third and the fourth generation.'*

I believe there's a general distinction between iniquity, transgression, and sin. Sin is the more general term. It simply means 'missing the mark'. The English word, sin, was a term used in archery. If you aimed for the target and missed, the official yelled out, "Sin!" Even if you were trying to hit the bull's-eye and missed, it was still considered a sin.

The Hebrew word for sin is *khattah*. The Greek word is *hamartano*, and it means 'not a witness.' *Martano* is where we get out English word martyr. Both *khattah* and *hamartano* mean 'to miss the mark,' whether you're aiming at it or not. When we sin, we're not being a witness of the nature of Jesus. Iniquity and transgression are both words which come under the general category of sin.

Transgression is a willful act of disobedience to a known law, whether secular or sacred. It's a purposed act, a premeditated act, a rebellious act. Yes, it's definitely sin, but it's an act that stems from deeper origins of thought and attitude. Transgression is when we know what God wants us to do, yet we're choosing not to do it. Iniquity is at the heart of all sin. It's that inner inclination which lies in the heart of all people because of their twisted, fallen nature. As a matter of fact, that's the definition of the word— 'perversity, moral evil, and twisted nature.' It's that core part that outs itself in sinful expression.

First Corinthians 13:6 says God's love *does not rejoice in iniquity.*... 'Rejoicing in' means 'having an inner approval and gladness over evil and calamity that happens to another person'. If you're a Christian, that iniquity is never worthy of our fleshly satisfaction. We shouldn't be rejoicing in things that grieve the heart of God.

## GOD GRIEVES OVER WHAT SIN DOES TO US

God's love has no pleasure in seeing a twisted and immoral heart reveal itself. It's not what He intended when He created man. Iniquity is always a destructive thing. Somewhere along the line we go down the ladder to more destruction in our soul. Maybe nobody is the wiser for what we did, maybe nobody was hurt, and everything seems fine; but something happens on the inside when we yield to any and every kind of sin.

It's like spilling battery acid on your clothes. You can wipe it all off and it looks like it's gone, but something is eating at you. Soon, you're walking down the street, and your clothes fall off because the battery acid has done a very good job of pulling apart the molecules and destroying that adhesion.

Iniquity does the same thing. That's why God hates sin. It's not that He's trying to keep us from anything; He doesn't want to see us destroyed. It's not His best for us, and it's not what He desires.

The Scripture says "God has no pleasure in the death of the wicked," even though judgment must be meted out on the soul that sins without faith in Christ Jesus.

**Ezekiel 33:11** *Say to them: 'As I live,' says the Lord God, 'I have no pleasure in the death of the wicked, but that the wicked turn from his way and live. Turn, turn from your evil ways! For why should you die, O house of Israel?'*

I hope you can hear the heart of the Lord in this verse. We may have had personal enemies when we were growing up, or people that did evil to our family. Listen, God created every soul. Every soul on the face of this planet was created by Him, and Jesus bore the sin of all mankind. If a person dies without Christ, it's a grievous thing to God. He knows the reality of eternity. God's love doesn't rejoice in iniquity.

**2 Peter 3:9** *The Lord is not slack concerning His promise, as some count slackness, but is longsuffering toward us, not willing that any should perish but that all should come to repentance.*

Is God trying to control people when He says this through the apostle Peter? No, because He's granted to every person free will. God will be reasonable, He'll work with our willingness, He'll bring to us the truth, but He'll not violate our free will, because true love doesn't violate another's will. Do we want people to be forced to love us? That's not real love. That's sheer obedience. Genuine love has this factor of a willing expression of care.

God desires that all come to repentance. Humbling ourselves before God is the best thing we can do because it releases all of God's good intentions toward us; yet still we fight it. We can say, "God doesn't understand. If I become

a Christian, I'm not going to be able to do this or do that."
With that thinking we're completely misunderstanding the
heart of God.

## WHEN AN ENEMY'S LIFE FALLS APART

'Rejoice in iniquity' means not so much the doing of
iniquity, as it has to do with being internally glad at seeing
the results of iniquity take its toll on someone. It's when you
say in your heart, "Look at that person, look at the kind of
life they have. They're getting what they deserve now, and
their whole life is falling apart. Good, I'm glad they're finally
getting theirs."

God's love isn't glad when a person's life falls apart. If I
want God's love ruling in my life, I need to line up my heart
with His and rethink this whole thing. A person controlled
by the love of God should grieve over another's calamity and
not gloat over the evil that's taken place.

Listen to these Old Testament Scriptures about having
this kind of attitude:

**Proverbs 24:17-18**
*[17] Do not rejoice when your enemy falls, And do not
let your heart be glad when he stumbles; [18] Lest the
LORD see it, and it displease Him, And He turn away
His wrath from him.*

The point of this is not to let the other person's evil lock
us up. The best thing we can do is put Jesus between us and
the other person. Let Jesus deal with us, and let Him deal
with them; no reaching around Jesus and grabbing for their
throat. Just let Him take care of it. It may seem like they're
getting away with everything, but it's not our concern. The
Lord will take care of it. He sees everything; He's gathering
evidence.

In talking to the surrounding nation of Edom through the prophet Obadiah, God says to them, as it reads in the Amplified Bible:

**Obadiah 1:12** *But you should not have gloated over your brother's day, the day when his misfortune came {and} he was made a stranger; you should not have rejoiced over the sons of Judah in the day of their ruin; you should not have spoken arrogantly in the day of their distress.*

Let's say that we've been very wise in how we've guided our life, family, and finances. We've paid off our house and have no debts. We've worked very hard to accomplish this. Then we happen to see our neighbor losing their house and being brought to nothing. Inside we think, "You know, those people weren't walking with wisdom. They just got what they deserved because they didn't plan. How unwise they were!"

Let me give a warning on this. That kind of heart will lead to some chastening from the Lord. While it may be true that God, in His own grace, allowed us to come to that point of freedom in our life, it doesn't mean we're smarter or more righteous than the other person. When we allow that kind of attitude in ourselves, it's not long before we're saying, like the self-righteous religious leader, "Lord, I thank you I'm not like that person. I even tithe on my salt and pepper." We're presenting to the Lord all our good deeds, and we look down on the sinner. Jesus condemns that.

It's right to be wise in what we do and we always are learning. But we have to be careful we don't look down upon our brother when calamity or distress comes upon them, gloating over them and saying, "Well, they just got what they deserved. They're deadbeats anyway." The Lord has a heart for the poor, the orphans, and those who are downcast. He heals the brokenhearted and binds up their wounds. Some of the Corinthian Christians were rejoicing in iniquity. There were infightings among themselves, and they were taking one another to court. One man was living with his stepmother in an incestuous relationship. But the church leaders were acting as if they would put up on their outdoor billboard, "We're the tolerant church." Paul was trying to spiritually wake them up by this epistle. God's love does not rejoice in iniquity, but it rejoices in the truth.

## REJOICING IN THE TRUTH

Let's now examine the second phrase of verse six: "[God's love] *rejoices in the truth.*" In other words, God's love rejoices when truth and right prevail.

Webster's 1828 Dictionary gives these definitions of the word 'true': 1. Conformable to fact; being in accordance with the actual state of things; 2. Genuine; pure; real; not counterfeit, adulterated or false; 3. Faithful; steady in adhering to friends, to promises, to a prince or to the state; loyal; not false, fickle or perfidious; 4. Free from falsehood.

Conformable to fact means that it conforms to facts and the actual state of things. Accurate facts are necessary to establish a standard of truth. When you go to the dollar store and pick up a ruler, guess what? It's actually twelve inches long. No matter how cheap the wood is, it's still twelve inches long. That size is a standard. Imagine if in each store you went to, the rulers varied a little bit depending on the kind of wood that was used.

Those standards of measurement are outside of ourselves; they're standards of truth, whether it's twelve inches, one mile, or one kilometer. When truth is only relative to the situation, relative to the culture, relative to our own philosophy of life, there's no constant standard. It's always changing, always morphing, always unstable and chaotic. There has to be a standard for truth outside of ourselves. If we're going to define truth as that which is conformable to fact, conformable to the actual state of things, then who sets that standard? I believe the standard is God Himself. What He tells us is the truth. What He says in His Word is the truth.

When you examine John's gospel and his general epistles in the New Testament, you find that he includes many references to this word 'truth.'

**John 1:14** *And the Word became flesh and dwelt among us, and we beheld His glory, the glory as of the only begotten of the Father, full of grace and truth.*

**John 4:23** *But the hour is coming, and now is, when the true worshipers will worship the Father in spirit and truth; for the Father is seeking such to worship Him.* *²⁴ God is Spirit, and those who worship Him must worship in spirit and truth.*

**John 8:32** *And you shall know the truth, and the truth shall make you free.*

Jesus was talking about truth based upon God's standard, not man's. Yet, I've heard this verse used in the world of psychology. The trouble is that so many times the psychological field determines what's true. It's not God's moral value; it's theirs. But according to the context in John's gospel, Jesus was referring to who God is and what He's presented though His Son as the truth.

**John 14:6** *Jesus said to him, "I am the way, the*

*truth, and the life. No one comes to the Father except through Me.*

The Holy Spirit is called the Spirit of truth by our Lord Jesus in John 14:17; 15:26; and 16:13:

**John 14:17** *the Spirit of truth, whom the world cannot receive, because it neither sees Him nor knows Him; but you know Him, for He dwells with you and will be in you.*

**John 15:26** *But when the Helper comes, whom I shall send to you from the Father, the Spirit of truth who proceeds from the Father, He will testify of Me.*

**John 16:13** *However, when He, the Spirit of truth, has come, He will guide you into all truth; for He will not speak on His own authority, but whatever He hears He will speak; and He will tell you things to come.*

When Jesus prayed to the Father in John 17:17, He said, *Sanctify them* [these disciples] *by Your truth; Your word is truth.* Then He says in verse 19: *And for their sakes, I sanctify Myself that they also may be sanctified by the truth.*

To be sanctified means 'to be cleansed and set aside for His special use'. The truth of the Lord (His perspective, how He sees it) is a cleansing thing in our life. We benefit greatly when we order our life according to His truth rather than the world's truth.

God's love *does not rejoice in iniquity but rejoices in the truth.* In living out our life as a Christian, we're faced every day with choices. We're surrounded with billboards, media, radio, television, and movies that seek to stir up the passions of our flesh. Unfortunately, it becomes a real challenge to walk according to what's right in God's eyes and not according to the peer pressure of our culture.

## TRUE JOY

*"...rejoice in the truth."* I believe that joy is the first outcropping of God's love. This is implied in Paul's epistle to the Galatian Christians:

**Galatians 5:22-23**
*[22] But the fruit of the Spirit is love, joy, peace, longsuffering, kindness, goodness, faithfulness, [23] gentleness, self-control. Against such there is no law.*

All nine of these descriptions of the fruit of the Spirit come forth independent of our outward circumstances. Paul begins the list with 'love' because it's the highest one. Some have said that all the rest of the descriptions--joy, peace, longsuffering, kindness, goodness, faithfulness, gentleness, and self-control--are the expressions of love. I have to agree when I examine 1 Corinthians 13:4-8. These expressions are all born out of God's love.

Joy is the very first expression of love. Why? Because when God's love impacts our lives, it gives us such a deep hope and freedom.

Joy is different in quality than happiness. Happiness is more conditioned by outward circumstance, but when joy rules our heart we know the Lord is in charge. We know He's going to take care of things. There's that inner quietness, not depending upon the outward circumstances. Love *rejoices in the truth*, rejoices when right and truth prevail. There are times when our flesh doesn't want to hear the truth; we'd rather hide the truth or skirt around the issue.

For instance, when tax time comes, some of us may wrestle with this. We don't want to be truthful, we don't want to be honest, and we want to hide what actually took place that year. We want to twist the facts and give half truths. But let me say this: every time we try to hide the truth, it gets more complicated. We can't keep up with our stories.

God's love *rejoices in the truth*. Sometimes we don't like it when people speak truth into our life, or when they're concerned about the direction we're going. They sit down with us in love and say, "Listen, I see these things going on in your life, and I read in the Bible that these things are listed as sin. Do you realize what you're doing?" That's speaking truth into someone's life in love. Sometimes we don't like to hear the truth because we're so used to having our own way.

## APPLYING THIS TO ALL OF OUR RELATIONSHIPS

Let's take a look at how these truths apply to marriage. Here's an illustration that may have some relevance. Let's say your husband is adamant that his idea is the way things are going to be done. He might say, "It has to be done this way, and we're putting out this much cash and it's going to unfold; it's going to be the best thing. I know you don't like it, but I know this is the way it should go." You have these alarm bells and whistles going off inside you. You're thinking, "I have a bad feeling about all this." So you gently try to warn him about the dangers of such a move.

Then you hear him say, "Well, I'm going to do it anyway." There can be this little hidden thing from the flesh that comes up in you and says, "Alright, I can't wait until he crashes and burns. That'll show him what an idiot he is." I tell you that God will deal with you in this, because that attitude isn't His heart.

On the other hand, there are times when your husband has truly sensed something from the Lord, and you don't want to go through the heartache and inconvenience of the process, and so you fight. The trouble is, this attitude will bring a division in your relationship. It's not that your husband is always right, and it's not that you, as his wife are always right. It's so important to make sure your heart is right before God, even though you don't understand what's going down. When it seems like you're losing control of everything that's happening, it's best to come together as husband and wife and start praying with each other. We have to spiritually close the ranks and circle the wagons as husband and wife. If we fail to do this, Satan is right there to divide our relationship as quickly as possible.

Those of us who have a family are trying to raise our children in a way that's respectful and honorable. Let's say our son is in school and there's this one child who's bullying him. We then give this counsel to our son: "Knock him out before he gets to you. Hit him in the nose, because when that blood starts flowing it's all over and you'll win; might is right."

So are we saying the Holy Spirit is telling us to train our son to hit first and ask questions later? There are ways to deal with bullies in a constructive way, but a punch in the nose to start with isn't the first place to go. It's hard raising children in our world today. We must be careful what we allow our children to watch on television, and what they see in the movies. Those images may set patterns that they'll follow in real life.

How would these truths apply in relationships with other people? Let's say we're going out to eat with someone who has invited us to dinner; we're single and they're single, it's kind of a date... sort of. It's just an initial meeting, and we start liking the person, they start liking us, there are little sparks, a little fireworks, a little chemistry going on, and we're pretty excited and starting to think about them all day long. Then we find out the person secretly went out with someone else and told us a false story why they weren't going to be available. All of the sudden these feelings of hurt, anger, frustration, depression, disappointment, and vengeance come up in us. "I hope they get in a wreck," we might think. Wait a minute; we have to check that. Maybe the Lord was protecting us from getting involved with them more seriously. Maybe it was God's answer to our prayer. Maybe they weren't the best one for us; they weren't going to be good for us. It's hard to walk in God's love, but it's possible. It has to happen from the inside out.

It's shocking how much influence the world's thinking has infiltrated us. But God is always pressing forward to cleanse us, change us, and to wash us of the defilement. As the Holy Spirit brings each of these areas to light, let's lift them to Him and ask Him to create in us a clean heart and to renew within us a right spirit.

Bob, Jeanne, Micah, and Jesse
after they moved to Phoenix, 1978

# CHAPTER 10

## ~~⊚~~ LOVE BEARS, BELIEVES, ~~⊚~~ HOPES, ENDURES ALL THINGS

Sometimes you just have to face your fears. For twenty-seven years I'd been terrified of being in water where I couldn't touch the bottom with my feet. I have vivid memories of swimming lessons at an early age that were disastrous. The phobia kept me from enjoying most water sports.

Now I was faced with a dilemma; we were moving from Oregon to Arizona. Backyard swimming pools were in many of those homes. The thought of my two young boys being in trouble in one of those pools, and not being able to save them forced me to confront the greatest fear of my life: that of drowning.

In a step motivated by love for my sons I signed up for adult beginner swim lessons at an indoor pool in Eugene, Oregon. I was determined to conquer this fear even if it killed me... which I thought might be a possibility.

The first few lessons were easy. I could touch the bottom of the pool. I figured that we'd gradually move down toward the deeper end and I'd build up my confidence step by step. But suddenly one night, my plan came crashing down.

The instructor said, "OK, everyone out of the pool." Then he headed straight for the diving pool. My heart almost stopped beating! I positioned myself at the back of the line, trying to build up some sense of courage. I kept thinking about my sons in trouble in a pool and not being able to save them. I thought, "I've got to conquer this. Lord, please help me."

One by one, those in front of me jumped in and then grabbed the pole that was held out by the instructor. Then it was my turn. I went catatonic on the edge of the pool. I couldn't get myself to jump. They all started encouraging me to go, offering every reasoning in the book. But in my mind, if I jumped, I was a dead man. By the time they realized I was not coming up, I thought, and they had to find someone to jump in after me I would have died drowning.

Still, the picture of my sons in trouble haunted me over and over. I just had to do something. I took the biggest breath I could hold (after all it would be a few minutes before someone would get down and fish me out) and launched out into the air.

In those milliseconds while in the air a thousand thoughts raced through my mind. "You idiot! You're going to die! It all comes to an end right here." I hit the water with my eyes closed tightly waiting for the inevitable. And to my extreme surprise I floated up to the top and felt the water around my ears. But I was afraid to open my eyes and have the reality forced upon me that I was in the middle of a body of water where I couldn't touch bottom.

Finally I reached out with my eyes closed, took a hold of the pole, and was brought to the side of the pool. I climbed out and everyone applauded. How humbling and yet exhilarating... until I found myself once again locked up in fear at the edge of the pool not able to jump again. It took less time to actually jump in this time and the same thing happened: I floated to the top.

I drove home that evening absolutely ecstatic and offering praise to the Lord for helping me to begin conquering this lifelong fear. Yet now, over thirty-five years later, when I approach a pool to go swimming, a little twinge rises up within me. The only thing I've found which overcomes that twinge is to dive head first into the pool. Afterward, I have no problem the rest of the day.

The purpose of this true anecdote is to show that my love for my sons compelled me to bear, believe, hope, and endure all of my fears through the power and love of God. First Corinthians 13:7 says love *bears all things, believes all things, hopes all things, endures all things.* Let's take a look at those four qualities and make some applications to our lives as married couples, as families, and in how we deal with one another.

## LOVE IS A COVERING

Let's begin with the phrase, love *bears all things.* Remember, when we say love, we're not talking about human love; we're talking about God's love. The word that's used here is the Greek word *agape*, which identifies God's unconditional love.

Love bears all things. When we first read "...bears all things" it's easy to think of 'putting up with something'. But it means much more than that. The Greek word Paul used is a word that has to do with a roof, in its root meaning. So the idea being communicated by Paul is that God's love covers all things. His love is a roof under which we live; a protection for us like a roof keeps out the rain. This phrase has to do with covering the faults and mistakes of others. Love bears all things.

God's love would rather be a healing agent for another's faults than look to tear down others by spreading around their problems. Galatians 6:1 says *Brethren, .if a man is overtaken in any trespass, you who are spiritual* [or led by the Spirit] *restore such a one in a spirit of gentleness, considering yourself lest you also be tempted.* Bearing with the faults of others is a quality of God's love: it's a healing agent rather than a destroying agent.

This word bear also means 'to bear or cover the offenses of others against yourself, to bear up under personal injury, insult or disappointment.' I think one of the hardest things for us to bear is when people spread lies about us. We can handle almost anything else, fire me from my job, wreck my car, whatever else, but when personal insults are spread around, it cuts to the core. Yet God's love seeks to be a covering for another's weaknesses or offenses.

The greatest news is that I don't have to try to work this up, and I don't have to beg God for it. This love is already in our hearts as Christians because this love in found in the Holy Spirit. It's in the tool box, so to speak.

Love bears all things as a covering. That's the kind of love Paul was talking about, the kind of love the Corinthian believers needed so desperately. It's the kind of love we need in our life. I like what the apostle Peter says in his first epistle:

**1 Peter 4:8** *And above all things have fervent love for one another, for "love will cover a multitude of sins."*

## ALL THINGS

Paul felt impressed by the Holy Spirit to include the phrase 'all things' behind every one of these four words. Notice he didn't write 'some things,' nor 'most things,' but 'all things.' He wrote it this way on purpose. He wanted them to understand everything was included. Love bears all things.

Go to a concordance and look up the phrase 'all things'. You will find it occuring 220 times in the King James Version of the Bible. The surprising thing is that 171 of those times are found in the New Testament. So if you want to do a nice devotional, find all the verses that include the phrase 'all things' and then print them out. Take your highlighter and mark every time it says *all things*.

## LOVE BELIEVES THE BEST FIRST

Let's look at the second phrase; love *believes all things*. This isn't saying that God's love is gullible or simplistic. Rather, it has to do with 'a reasoning out' and 'a holding to' the truth. Actually, the phrase *believes all things* means that God's love is ever ready to believe the best of every person, ready to believe the best first, rather than the opposite. The laws of our country are based upon the premise that you're innocent until proven guilty. For the Christian, this should always be the case. A person is innocent first before being proven guilty. God's love is ever ready to believe the best of every person because it trusts; it never loses faith.

This is how God deals with us. We may not think of ourselves as being very good Christians right now. Things have happened that we're ashamed of; we've not maintained our promises to God. We've been living with a bad attitude and haven't been doing the things we used to do when we were walking in the fear of God.

How does God look at us now? According to what we know from this chapter, God believes the best about us. He isn't done with us. Our failing didn't surprise Him; it was in the file when He adopted us. God knows all things about us ahead of time. We don't know how that works because we certainly make free will choices; but God even knows our choices. God even knows the choices we would have made and what the ramifications of those choices would have been. It's important to relate to God as He reveals Himself to be in His Word, rather than bringing our ideas upon Him.

God believes the best about us first. He calls us to do the same with everyone, including our spouse, our children and our parents. When we take this truth, *love believes all things*, and apply it to God and to His Word, it causes us to take what God says at face value and trust His Word implicitly.

Rather than scrutinizing everyone we meet, the first reaction, when controlled by God's love, is to believe the best about them first. That's challenging because as time goes on, we get set in our patterns of how we view others. This is difficult for those who've been deeply hurt by others, Unfortunately, as we've considered before, a victim mentality can arise that sabotages every relationship, even if it was a healthy relationship in the beginning.

## LOVE RESTS UPON GOD'S PROMISES

Let's look at love *hopes all things.* This is more than positive thinking, or having a positive mental attitude. That kind of philosophy is based on man's ability to remain positive. What we're referring to is how God's love hopes all things. This is something of divine origin, something that's all together different in quality from human hope.

The word hope as it's used here means having a strong, confident assurance of what will unfold in God's timing and purpose. No matter if we lose our job, if we lose our house, if things are radically adjusted in our lives, we hope in Him; we know that God is in charge, and He's going to work out all things according to His purposes. We hold on to Him rather than the circumstances.

Instead of focusing on the circumstances, we need to put our faith in God. Our faith is anchored upon who God is and what He has promised. There's a resting of our entire life upon what He has said and how He's going to work out all things.

### Romans 8:28-29

<sup>28</sup> *And we know that all things work together for good to those who love God, to those who are the called according to His purpose.* <sup>29</sup> *For whom He foreknew, He also predestined to be conformed to*

*the image of His Son, that He might be the firstborn among many brethren.*

One of the ways God uses with 'all things' is to work on our character. It's easy to be a Christian when everything is going fine, when the sun is shining, the car is full of gas, our car is paid off, we've got only $20,000 left on the house mortgage; life is good. We just got that raise on our job, our children are doing well in school, there's not much challenge in our lives. Then comes the pink slip at work, letting us know our job has been outsourced. Next, we discover that all of our retirement investments have lost their value. We've nothing left, and our circumstances start unraveling like a bad sweater.

What kind of character has God built in us? When things go bad, that's when true character will start coming out. It's not that we have to go through those things and create trouble for ourselves. Trouble will come on its own. But God says, "I'll stand with you, and I'll show you My power."

## LOVE ENDURES ALL THINGS

Do you know that every single one of the miracles Jesus performed was done during a time of desperation for those folks? They wouldn't have seen the act as a miracle if there hadn't been desperation first.

We want God to do miracles in our lives, but we don't want to be desperate first. We'd rather say to Him, "Just bless me while I'm doing fine." We're like a child that wants everything. God's love never gives up on us; it doesn't lose heart or give in because of discouragement. Have we ever said to Him, "I can't handle this?" Have we ever had a trial so hard we say, "God, I'd just rather You kill me than go through this?"

Sometimes illnesses can put us into that mind set, sometimes children can bring us to that, and sometimes a bad marriage puts us right there. But listen: God's love endures all things. To endure means 'to persevere with a joyful expectation.' It doesn't get caught up looking back and becoming lost in the failures of the past. It presses onward. This quality of God's love holds its ground when the temptation is great to no longer believe or hope. Don't let your past failures block your forward motion in Him.

**2 Timothy 2:10** *Therefore I endure all things for the sake of the elect, that they also may obtain the salvation which is in Christ Jesus with eternal glory.*

Paul endured because he kept the goal before him. It gave him purpose, passion, and perseverance. God's purpose for endurance is not for us to tough it out, but for us to minister to others.

### Philippians 4:11-13
*[11] Not that I speak in regard to need, for I have learned in whatever state I am, to be content: [12] I know how to be abased, and I know how to abound. Everywhere and in all things I have learned both to be full and to be hungry, both to abound and to suffer need. [13] I can do all things through Christ who strengthens me.*

When Paul writes "I can do all things," he wasn't implying that we can accomplish whatever we dream up. He was using this phrase 'do all things,' meaning 'to endure all things'. I can endure anything that comes my way as long as Christ gives me the strength. That's the key. It's not my strength, but it's His strength working in me by His love and by His Holy Spirit.

This is a great Scripture for our economy right now. *I know how to be abased* means 'I've watched God work in times where I've had nothing, and I know the joy that I can have in my spirit, even though I've lost everything'. We also know that in times of abundance, God is with us to give us perspective and to keep our wits about us.

The things Paul writes concerning God's love were directly related to issues that were going on in the Corinthian congregation. All of verse seven, *bears all things, believes all things, hopes all things and endures all things*, applied to issues going on in the church of Corinth. They needed God's love controlling their lives.

Carnality and pride were the culprits within this group of believers. They were priding themselves in their superior knowledge of spiritual things, but they didn't seem to notice they weren't living out God's love in everyday life. For instance, Paul, in 1 Corinthians 6 told them:

**1 Corinthians 6:7-8**
*⁷ Now therefore, it is already an utter failure for you that you go to law against one another. Why do you not rather accept wrong? Why do you not rather let yourselves be cheated? ⁸ No, you yourselves do wrong and cheat, and you do these things to your brethren!*

It's easy to come into a group and tell things to try making people think we're spiritual. But how do we live when no one's looking? What's going on behind the scenes? What we live in private is our real theology.

It's important to bring our Christianity right into where we live because our children know the difference. If we don't want our children to hate Christianity and hate church, then we're not to be living differently at church than we live at home. It doesn't mean we're perfect. But when we do sin at home, we must follow through and ask their forgiveness. We need to use it as an object lesson. We can't just think, "Well, they'll get over it."

## HOW THESE ATTRIBUTES BLESS
## A MARRIAGE

Let's take a deeper look at how verse seven shows itself in the three life situations of marriage, family, and relationships. God's love *bears all things*. Remember, the word 'bear' means 'a covering, to hover over, and to protect'. If you're a husband, God has called you to 'bear all things' concerning your family. He wants you to be the one that's overseeing, watching over, protecting, and covering your family spiritually. What does that look like? Do you have to give them Bible studies every night? No, not necessarily, but you do have to pray for your family regularly.

You have to be an example to your family, to take who you are and what you're going through and let God use it to touch your family, and especially your spouse. Jesus said in John 17, *I sanctify Myself for their sakes.* Jesus was God incarnate, yet there were things that He purposely did to affect His disciples. There are things you need to do as a husband to sanctify your life before God. You must watch what you're doing, and how you're talking for the sake of your family and your wife.

It's the same with the wife toward her husband. Are you bearing all things concerning him? Do you talk about your husband to others in a way that's derogatory? Sure, you may be having conflicts at home, but do you frequently run him down in front of other people because you're feeling so depressed about things? When you push him down in the dirt and say he's a clueless old man, that's not God's love. That's your flesh speaking and it'll come back on you with interest. Love bears all things, love believes all things, believes the best first.

If you're married, and your wife is having difficulty, it's your job as a husband not to control her, but to sit and listen. The odds are she doesn't want your answer; she wants someone to listen because she's pouring out her heart. You aren't to be the Bible answer man. Just listen, and then you're to tell her what you heard her say. Be careful with this. You need to make sure you get it right.

Gals, sometimes you want your husband to open up and talk to you. You see that he's bothered by something. You say to him, "What's wrong?" He says, "Nothing's wrong." You say back, "What's really wrong?" He returns with, "I don't want to talk about it."

If this is how the conversation is going, don't get the crowbar out and try to pry it out of him. The best thing you can do is intercede and pray to the Lord for him. You know him more than anyone else and You know when he's going through tough times and is frustrated.

Love 'hopes all things.' Remember, 'hopes all things' is hoping in how the Lord is going to use all that's going on. When everything starts falling apart in our marriage, we're to say, "God, I want You to intervene here. You're stronger than we are. I don't know how this is going to turn out, but I've got to keep my eyes on You, not on the faults of my spouse, and not on this bad situation." That's God's love in action.

'Endures all things' isn't based on sheer will power to work out our marriage issues; it has to do with letting God give us the strength to make it through life's difficulties. The best thing we can do is to pray together even if we're mad at each another. It's hard to pray with someone we're mad at because everything in us wants to pray for God to nail them. "God, You know we love You so much; just teach my husband how much he's offended me." We shouldn't have that mind set if we want to bring healing into our marriage.

## HOW THESE ATTRIBUTES BLESS OTHERS

What about the family? There are times when we have deadlines, and our children aren't cooperating. We then need to go to the Lord and say, "I need Your love, to love these children; because right now they're being very selfish, and I'm about to lose my patience. So God, please help me regroup and come back into the situation with a clear mind , Your love, and some kind of a strategy."

We're not to come at them in anger, yelling and screaming, thinking we're going to control them by our anger. We're a huge mountain to our little ones, and when we come in with our big booming voice, it'll have a definite effect upon them. But, does it bring them closer to us? Rather, it puts the fear of dad in them, and they keep their distance. It doesn't mean we have to be soft and sweet with them all the time. But it does mean we have to let God's love control us regarding our children.

Children are naturally dawdlers; their sense of time isn't our sense of time. We have to think ahead and prepare them. If we've a deadline to meet, we've got to think ahead and start preparing them earlier. Move them along so that they'll fit into the time limitation. It's hard, but it's not impossible; God's love will help.

Finally, in our relationships with other people, when we hear gossip at the office, we're not to pass it on. This is an application of love 'bears all things'. When we hear rumors about someone, usually what we're hearing is embellished and not even the whole truth. We spread the burden of forgiveness when we pass along someone else's sinful action to another person. All of the sudden, they now look at them entirely different through what they have heard from us.

What if this person has repented, gotten it cleared up and gone on? But this other person always looks at him or her through that sin they've heard about because we've had a hand in spreading it on. We need to cover it, to bear all things; it's important. That's how we would want to be treated. Believe the best first. Hope in the Lord's promise and purpose for everything that happens. Does all of this seem impossible to put into practice? Take heart. Nothing's too hard for the Lord. His Holy Spirit is poised to bring this about in our lives. Our part is to yield and invite Him to make a new start. He'll do the work in us that we might let His love flow through us.

My dad, Elmer Claycamp, at age 85

# CHAPTER 11

## LOVE NEVER FAILS

Those three simple words, I LOVE YOU, can change a relationship. Looking back on the days as I was growing up, I don't recall being very emotionally close to my parents. They had many difficult issues to deal with and there wasn't that special bonding time between us. I knew they loved me in their own way, but they never said those words to me verbally; I sometimes wonder if it was how things were done in their generation. But for me, those words were important to hear. So I didn't have that life experience of what a close relationship with my dad or mom could be like.

It wasn't until my dad was in his 80's that we finally made a breakthrough and began to communicate with the words, "I love you." It was amazing; it was like he became a different person and we entered a new phase in our relationship as father and son. This led to him eventually wanting to have me take care of him in his last years.

I got to know my father all over again. My wife and sons developed a close relationship with him as well. It was almost as if he was a completely different man from what I remember during those earlier years. My wife and I felt we had a mandate from the Lord to 'bless his last years' although we didn't know how long that would be. After only eighteen months, he passed away peacefully at age eighty-six in our home. He was ready to meet his Lord and the angels came to escort him into the Lord's presence on that Wednesday morning.

I remember having a sense from the Holy Spirit to my spirit after his passing, giving me the release from that mandate. The chapter was now closed. We had done what was set before us to do.

## QUESTIONING GOD'S LOVE

First Corinthians 13:8 begins with three words, *love never fails*. This is the 16th attribute of God's love we find in verses 4-8. I like how the Amplified Bible translates this verse:

**1 Corinthians 13:8** *Love never fails [never fades out or becomes obsolete or comes to an end].*

Take a look at the current crises in marriages, even among Christians. There's a general lack of love all across the board. It affects our society, it affects our children, and it affects the future of our country. We can't patch it up with legislation; we can't think that it'll go away if we just modify the behavior. Lack of love is huge, and the cost is detrimental.

Jesus promised that He'd never leave us nor forsake us. So why do bad things happen? If He promised never to leave us or forsake us, couldn't He have stopped that evil event from taking place? Couldn't He have blocked that situation? Couldn't He have provided when we needed the provision? We all ask those kinds of questions at times.

When we make circumstances or our perception of what is going on around us the main proof of whether God loves us or not, we're absolutely walking in a lie. The Bible, God's Word, doesn't support that theory. God desires to take care of us and to meet our needs, but somewhere along the line, we can make circumstances the validation of whether God loves us or not. We come up with these choice gems to throw at God as if He's at fault.

The reality is this: sin is in the world. People aren't going to throw a parade for us because we moved into town and we're a Christian. Just because things are working out our way doesn't mean God is super pleased with the way we're living. On the other hand, just because things are going terribly wrong doesn't mean God is mad at us or is putting us under His chastening.

Now, it's possible that if we're living in sin and God is starting to take the wheels off our chariot, He's trying to get our attention. But He's not up there like an angry judge with a gavel in His hand ready to bring it down upon us every time we get out of line. Maybe that's how our earthly father was, but it's not how our heavenly Father is.

## EVERLASTING LOVE

God's love is constant and everlasting. He never fails. His love never comes to an end. God's love is eternal and He will not lie to us about His love. God loves all of us with His everlasting love, even though we live out our life in wickedness. It grieves God's heart to see a soul pour themselves into a wicked life. There's such destruction in a sinful life.

How do I know that God's love is everlasting? Because the Bible tells us.

**Jeremiah 31:3** *The LORD has appeared of old to me, saying: "Yes, I have loved you with an everlasting love; Therefore with lovingkindness I have drawn you."*

Here's a simple definition of 'everlasting': 'From the vanishing point to the vanishing point'. When we look down a set of railroad tracks, it seems like they come together at the end. If we try to find that point where they seemingly meet, we will go on for miles and miles. God's everlasting love is 'from the vanishing point to the vanishing point.' After we meet Jesus face to face, His love toward us will not increase, nor will it decrease. He loves us with an everlasting love.

Somehow we think that once we get around the bases, cross home plate, and count the runs, we're finished. God's love is done. We've made it to heaven. But it's not that way. God loves us right now with an everlasting love. His love never fails. That's why Paul says God's love is so excellent. It's to be the focus of our life, rather than all the special talents or gifts we have.

**Romans 8:28** *And we know that all things work together for good to those who love God, to those who are the called according to His purpose.*

So when bad things happen in our life, does it negate this Scripture? We have to take the bad things that happen and put it up against this Scripture. It'll give perspective to the evil that may be currently going on in our life.

The fascinating truth about this New Covenant in the blood of Jesus Christ is that God is always working. He's constantly working on my behalf so that I don't have to work. He wants me to rest, He wants me to trust, He wants me to relax and enjoy Him without trying to gain His acceptance. Sometimes that's a major trial because we don't feel like He loves us. We put so much dependence upon what's happening around us, or what we think should happen, or what we think should not happen, and we block all that God wants to do.

He can take whatever we throw at Him and turn it around. He can take all our broken pieces and create a beautiful mosaic. I have to trust God for that because I don't feel it immediately, but I'll see it at the end.

Romans 8:35-39 contains a very important teaching about God's love never failing.

**Romans 8:35-39**
*[35] Who shall separate us from the love of Christ? Shall tribulation, or distress, or persecution, or*

*famine, or nakedness, or peril, or sword? [36] As it is written: "For Your sake we are killed all day long; We are accounted as sheep for the slaughter."[37] Yet in all these things we are more than conquerors through Him who loved us. [38] For I am persuaded that neither death nor life, nor angels nor principalities nor powers, nor things present nor things to come, [39] nor height nor depth, nor any other created thing, shall be able to separate us from the love of God which is in Christ Jesus our Lord.*

It's interesting that Paul said 'who' and not 'what' shall separate us from the love of Christ. Who can come against us to block us from God's love? Do we think it's Satan? Do we think it's ourselves, our failures, our broken promises, or our bad witness in times past? The answer is no one, and then Paul goes on and draws upon things that can cause us to question His love.

Even though the Christian is enveloped in the love of God, they'll still experience tribulation, distress, persecution, famine, nakedness, peril, and even the sword. By the way, those things are happening around the world right now to other believers. maybe even to you who are reading this book. Paul then brings in this Scripture from Isaiah as proof: *For Your sake we are killed all day long; We are accounted as sheep for the slaughter.* That being true, Paul says in verse 37, *Yet in all these things we are more than conquerors through Him who loved us.*

## RESTING IN HIS LOVE

How in the world do we keep our perspective when these things are going on in our lives? *Through Him who loved us.* Jesus stands with us in the fire, so there's no rush to get out because He's with us. There's a peace; there's a comfort there. I don't think Paul could have included anything more in these passages. They cover position, people and places. God wants us to rest in Him, so that we can enjoy life in Him; so that we can enjoy Him; so that we can enjoy our brethren, and not be so worried about ourselves. We have such a hard time resting in that as Christians.

If we're married, God desires for us to be secure in Jesus so that we can love our spouse with holy, complete love, and not be so worried about what we're getting out of it. One of the biggest problems in marriages is selfishness, and it breaks down the marriage unit. God's love is holy, pure, healing, and restoring.

In the family our children are craving our love. We have to understand what their different needs are because one child has a different kind of need than the next child. We can't have a cookie-cutter approach to each of the children. We can't force them into a mold. If we do, we're not loving them in the way that'll have the greatest impact for their good.

We should spend not only corporate time together as a family; we need individual time with our children. It would be beneficial to take them over to an ice cream shop. Then over a simple hot fudge sundae, just love them, talk with them and enjoy them. That always brightens their day. They may not be able to understand what we're doing, but they'll love the way it feels. It becomes a time of bonding.

Now, maybe our children live far away from us. Maybe they've hardened their heart against us. How did that happen? Maybe we cut them off all the time, maybe we tried to control them, maybe we were always telling them what to do, and we weren't truly listening to them. The goal is always to love them, and open up the communication lines again so the wall can begin to come down. Then maybe we can connect with that 'little kid' we used to know.

We should let our children know that our love for them won't fail even if they should go into a rebellious phase. In love, we'll tell them the truth concerning their waywardness, yet we're to listen more than we talk. A lot of times they'll say things for sheer shock value. Sure, it's a challenge. They'll go through a lot of phases as they try to piece together their world. But it gives us the opportunity to know how to pray for them.

God's love compels us to live for Him. When we lock in on the reality of God's love for us, it has a profound effect upon our life. Rather than working to get something from God, we find ourselves motivated from within to serve Him without even thinking about it. God's love compels us to live for Him.

### 2 Corinthians 5:14-15 New Living Translation
[14] *Either way, Christ's love controls us. Since we believe that Christ died for all, we also believe that we have all died to our old life.* [15] *He died for everyone so that those who receive his new life will no longer live for themselves. Instead they will live for Christ, who died and was raised for them.*

Understand that when our hearts are stirred by the love of God to love others, not everyone is going to necessarily love us back. It happened with the apostle Paul. He wrote in 2 Corinthians 12:15 *And I will very gladly spend and be spent for your souls; though the more abundantly I love you, the less I am loved.*

This may describe what's been going on in our family with our older children. The more we love them, the more they think we're so ignorant. Well, God is asking us to bear

it. We're not to take it personally. We're to catch it and love
them back because, guess what... God did that with us.

He loved us completely, and the more He loved us, the
more we rejected Him. We didn't want it, we were afraid of
it. We pushed it away; we threw all of our arguments at it.
And when we read this verse, we hear Jesus saying through
the apostle Paul's words: *And I will very gladly spend and be
spent for your souls; though the more abundantly I love you,
the less I am loved.*

Some people are hard to love, they're hard to get close
to, and it's like trying to pet a porcupine. It hurts. You go to
love them, and you get poked, and then you want to throw a
rock at them. But we're called to love, even if it hurts, even
if there's no love requited. But it has to be the Holy Spirit in
us that gives us the strength to continue to walk in His love.

In our marriage our spouse may have shut off his or her
heart from us, and we can't seem to regain it. Everything
we do is now looked upon as suspicious; no matter how
hard we try, it never seems to work. God isn't calling us
to love conditionally, as long as it works; God is calling
us to love unconditionally whether it seems to work or
not. It's the same love with which He loved us. He loved
us while we were in sin, while we were practicing sin,
while we were in immorality, while we were in thievery,
while we were in our addictions. God absolutely loved us,
to draw us to Himself because His is an everlasting love.

## GOD'S LOVE LOOKS LIKE JESUS

Jesus is the express image of God's love. If we want
to see how we're to love, all we have to do is spend time
considering our Lord Jesus—especially in the Gospel of
John. The disciples had walked with Jesus for at least three
years. They'd heard so many of His teachings. They had

watched Him minister to countless numbers of people. After all that time here is what Jesus says to them:

**John 13:34-35**
*³⁴ A new commandment I give to you, that you love one another; as I have loved you, that you also love one another. ³⁵ By this all will know that you are My disciples, if you have love for one another.*

What does this love look like? It looks like Jesus, His heart, His truth, His quality of love. Sometimes Jesus' love expressed itself in sternness when He encountered self-righteousness. He caused some trouble with the Pharisees when He told them the truth, even though it made them mad. Seeing how Jesus loves is our greatest example, our highest example because He's the express image of God's love.

In Revelation 3:19, Jesus said, *As many as I love, I rebuke and chasten. Therefore be zealous and repent.*

Love doesn't turn the eye away and say it doesn't matter. Sometimes people say it's intolerance when you confront sin. True Biblical tolerance is when you choose to cover someone's sin while they are being worked on rather than spreading the news all around. Yet many conclude that it's politically incorrect or intolerant to rebuke a brother or sister for sinful behavior.

I agree that one can be careless in how they confront a sinning brother or sister in Christ. The problem comes when the rebuke is given in a spirit of pride and arrogance. Then you are in as much sin as they are. Galatians 6:1-5 addresses this very thing:

**Galatians 6:1-5**
*¹ Brethren, if a man is overtaken in any trespass, you who are spiritual restore such a one in a spirit of gentleness, considering yourself lest you also be*

*tempted. ² Bear one another's burdens and so fulfill*
*the law of Christ. ³ For if anyone thinks himself to be*
*something, when he is nothing, he deceives himself.*
*⁴ But let each one examine his own work, and then*
*he will have rejoicing in himself alone, and not in*
*another. ⁵ For each one shall bear his own load.*

If we see a brother or sister becoming overtaken in a
particular sin, what do we do? If we're truly led by the Spirit,
our goal is to restore them to Jesus. We're not to condemn
them, or throw them away; we're to approach them in a spirit
of gentleness considering ourselves lest we also be tempted.

"Bear one another's burdens" means that we come under
the yoke with them; if they are struggling under the weight
of what is going on in their life, we, as a fellow Christian,
are to come along side them and put our neck under the yoke
with them and help lift it up. This is so different than saying
to them, "Look at you. What kind of a Christian are you? If
you were a real Christian, you'd put your eyes on Jesus and
you wouldn't be in this shape."

If that's our heart toward them, we're in line for some
chastening from the Lord. Bear one another's overload is
what is meant in this verse. We're not to take that burden
completely off of them so they don't have any responsibility.
We're to bear their overload and so fulfill the law of Christ.

There's a personal balance in this counsel. We're to be
sensitive to what's going on in the lives of our brethren, but
we're also to be responsible before the Lord for our own walk.
It's amazing to hear stories of pastors who dedicate their lives
to help other people, and yet they let the rules go for their own
life, and end up in immorality or some other sin.

# LOVE THAT NEVER GIVES UP

In our relationships with others, whether we're married, whether it's with our children, our parents, our grandparents, or with people we encounter day to day, God has called us to have a love that never gives up, never quits, and never comes to an end. We have to go to Him to be refilled after we pour out His love to others.

There may come a time when we'll need to care for our parents. They may start going into dementia and forget important things and then keep telling us the same things over and over again. It can wear us down. In those times we have to go back to God and say, "I need Your grace; I not only need to be refilled with Your love, I need a constant filling. As much as You're pouring in, it seems like the same is going out every moment. I'm just worn out, Lord. I pray You refresh me, renew me and fill me with Your love. Help me to love them in their last days. Lord, there's going to come a time when they aren't going to be here, and I want to finish well. I want to have a clear conscience, and I want to have that chapter closed, knowing that I've done everything I could within my ability." God will be faithful to help us and give the strength, courage, and resources to care for them.

Since God's love is everlasting and never gives up, we have a tremendous hope as His children. He fills us with His love and it'll absolutely change our lives. If we think we're ready to give up on loving others, God is right there to shore us up and refill us. Ask and we shall receive. Seek and we shall find. Knock and the door will be opened to us.

# CHAPTER 12

# ~~ THE GREATEST OF THESE ~~
# IS LOVE

Before I trusted Christ for my salvation, I was involved in the occult and spiritism. The rule of my life had become, 'the more mystical and unusual, the more it must be true'. My girlfriend (now my wife) and I would put ourselves in many situations of absolute demonic surroundings.

After we surrendered our lives to Jesus, there was still this left over mind set of mysticism that brought confusion and downright heretical thinking. I remember trying so hard to hear the voice of the Spirit to get a prompting on when to turn right or turn left as I walked down the street.

It all came to a head one sunny morning in Portland, Oregon. As I was on one of my experimental walks I came across an accident in the middle of the road. It was the old utility truck my Christian friends were using at our house. My friend Michael had been driving in downtown Portland when he said the Lord told him to drive with his eyes closed. This would be the ultimate test of obedience and relying upon the Spirit's direction, he thought.

We were so zealous to be obedient to what we thought were the Spirit's promptings that we checked our common sense at the door. Well, Michael ran into a parked car with that big truck. Then he concluded that God must have wanted him to talk to the owner of the car he ran into since he believed he was being led by the Spirit in the first place. It was right after that when God, in His mercy, put us into contact with a sound Christian youth ministry that grounded us in true faith and the Word of God.

I mention this anecdote because sometimes believers can think that manifestations of the Spirit are more important than anything else. But the real litmus test is this: am I walking regularly, daily, in the love of God? The very last verse of chapter 13 says, *"and now abide faith, hope, love, these three; but the greatest of these is love."* God desires for us to be saturated with His love, and there's a purpose why the Lord directed Paul to write the things he did here in chapter 13.

## TESTED BY LIFE

Time and time again, we're tested with how people treat us, and we're tested by circumstances of life. Our faith gets tested and sometimes our feelings don't line up with what we know to be true in our mind.

Sometimes we'll try to pretend that it's not happening and go on with life, but things still build up on the inside. Sometimes we'll turn to medications to try to anesthetize the depression and feelings. Sometimes we go off into wrong relationships with others to try to block out the confusion and pain. God wants us to turn to Him.

When we're feeling like we're losing our grip, that's not the time to turn away from God. That's the time to run to Him, fall down on our knees and say, "God, I need Your help because You know what's going on. You know the shape I'm in; You know more than I know, You know why and what to do about it. I need You to fill my life with Your love, peace, and joy. Put me in the eye of the hurricane, Lord, so that I'm not spun by life's circumstances. Put me in that peace that surpasses all understanding and help me hear Your voice to know my next step. I need the grace to make it through to the end of the day, and to end up with hope."

Verse 13 says. *"And now abide faith, hope and love these three..."*. These three, faith, hope, and love, are some of the most important qualities of our Christian life here during our pilgrimage on earth. When we get our eyes off of what the Lord has promised to us, off of the hope that He's set before us, and off of the love of God, we always end up in trouble.

We've been called to live by faith, live in faith, to live according to faith; our hope is founded on the promises of who He is, how He's revealed Himself to be, and the promises He's made to us. His love is even more important than faith and hope. Why? Because love lasts beyond this life. Faith is for this life here on earth. Once we see the Lord, our faith has been completed. We're not going to need faith after we're already changed and we're with the Lord for the rest of eternity.

We're not going to need to keep holding onto the hope of the gospel when we meet the Lord because we'll be with Him. Our hope will be fulfilled. But love will continue on forever, and we'll be enjoying and experiencing God's love in its full measure for the rest of eternity. That's why God's love excels all. That's why the greatest of these is love.

## LOVE IS GREATER THAN GIFTS OF THE SPIRIT

First Corinthians 13 is like the meat between the two slices of bread of a sandwich. One slice of bread is chapter 12 and the other slice of bread is chapter 14. The important part is not the bread; the important part is the meat. Chapter 12 to 14 is a section where Paul wanted to give some clarity and understanding regarding the gifts of the Holy Spirit which are given to believers. God's love is the prime motivating force behind the distribution and exercising of those gifts.

This last section of 1 Corinthians 13 is Paul's reminder to the Corinthian believers that even the most glorious gifts of God's Spirit are less in benefit compared to God's love. Those gifts are temporary in nature. They're for this life only, whereas God's love is eternal in nature.

When we look at the nine spiritual gifts listed in 1 Corinthians 12, understand there are other gifts mentioned in other epistles. We find some of them listed in Romans 12. There are yet others which are included in Ephesians 4, as well as in 1 Peter 4. To easily remember their locations in the New Testament, we can think of two numbers, 12 and 4: 1 Corinthians 12, Romans 12, Ephesians 4, and 1 Peter 4.

The purpose of the gifts of the Spirit has to do with our service to our Lord—power for service, effective service, and fruitful service in the Lord. The fruit of the Spirit has to do with our character change—love, joy, peace, longsuffering, gentleness, goodness, meekness, faithfulness, self-control. The Holy Spirit wants to take control of our heart and change us from glory to glory into the image of our Lord.

The fruit of the Spirit, I believe, is more important than the gifts of the Spirit. The gifts of the Spirit are absolutely needful for the church today, but what trumps the gifts of the Spirit is God's love. That's what Paul presents in 1 Corinthians 13. We don't want to lessen the importance and need for the gifts of the Spirit in our life, marriage, family, relationships, or even in the workplace.

Spiritual gifts aren't merely for prayer meetings. They are supposed to be a part of our everyday life. Looking through the book of Acts, we see the operation of those gifts of the Spirit; we see them exercised in everyday life situations when the believers were interacting with others. They were not always manifested when the brethren were cloistered in one little room. True, that happened the first time in Acts 2, but the rest of the time the believers were involved with the lives of other people, we see those gifts of the Spirit being used.

## POWER GIFTS

The nine gifts of the Spirit found in chapter 12 can be grouped into three categories. There are gifts that are called power gifts, gifts that are called discernment gifts, and gifts that are called vocal gifts. In the power gift category we have the gift of faith, the gift of miracles, and gifts of healings. The gift of faith is a special working of the Holy Spirit upon our heart where we absolutely 'know that we know that we know.' These gifts are distributions of God. They aren't something we manufacture, or even try to work up and get ourselves into an emotionally frenzy.

In our marriage, we need to ask God to give us those gifts which are needful to our situation. Sometimes it's going to take a miracle to straighten out our marriage. That's when we pray, "God, give to me the gift of faith; if You really want to do this work in our marriage, then You're going to have to work a miracle. Please give me the gift of faith."

We're going to need the gift of faith to believe God can change our heart, the heart of our spouse, or even the hearts of our children. When our parents are losing their faculties and we're being pressed to step in and care for them, and we don't know what the strategy is, that's when we need this special gift of faith

You don't have to be in a church setting, or in a church service to receive this gift; you don't have to be on a short-term mission. It's for everyday life because God goes with us in those everyday things. We can ask the Lord to give us whichever power gift we may need for that day, whether it's the gift of faith, the gift of miracles, or gifts of healings.

## DISCERNMENT GIFTS

The second category of spiritual gifts is called the discernment gifts. These gifts are the word of wisdom, the word of knowledge, and discernment of spirits. The word of wisdom is different than having general wisdom and understanding on how to deal with things. When Paul used the phrase 'the word of' and applied it to the word 'wisdom' he was implying it was a special application to a special situation. In other words, God puts forth a sense of what to do in the midst of that particular situation which we didn't have the wisdom to do before. We didn't have the experience base to draw upon, but all of the sudden it made sense and was the right thing at the right time in the right way.

The word of knowledge is not just knowing facts and figures and memorizing the encyclopedia; it has to do with the Holy Spirit giving us insight into a situation that was previously not known by us beforehand. It's when God wants to call out a particular situation and bring it to life so that He can move in that circumstance. There might be times when we are amongst believers who have gathered for prayer, where words of knowledge will come forth. The statements address areas in someone's life where the Lord is trying to work but the person is blocking Him by some specific sins to which they are yielding. A few details are mentioned but nobody in the group knows who is being addressed, except the person to whom it applies.

What is it like to have the Holy Spirit put a word of knowledge upon our heart? Some have described it as the Spirit giving a very deep impression upon the heart, and then that overall sense is spoken out in faith into the small group setting. That's one way the word of knowledge can be seen in operation.

There are times when we don't know what the trouble is with our children. Their behavior has turned a little strange, so unlike how they normally act. It's good for us to go to the Lord in prayer at that time and say, "Lord, give me insight. Give me the word of knowledge about what's going on in their life so I can minister to them and pray intelligently."

It's not wrong to ask God to move in those practical little ways; that's why we're given gifts of the Holy Spirit. Sometimes we put it off saying, "Well, I don't want to get weird." But we forget that God wants to help us in every small way with our families, our marriages, and in all our relationships. Whatever we're doing He goes with us— whether we're working, vacationing, or even out hunting.

The gift of the discerning of spirits is a strong inner sense from the Holy Spirit that what is going on around us is not of a godly origin; there's something diabolic with it. An illustration of the discerning of spirits in action was when Jesus said to Peter, "Get behind Me, Satan! For you aren't mindful of the things of God, but the things of men" (Mark 8:33). This was spoken to Peter when he was trying to discourage Jesus from going to the cross. Jesus revealed that the origin of Peter's thinking was not merely Peter being concerned about the Lord's future; it was something even more diabolical.

## VOCAL GIFTS

The third category of spiritual gifts is referred to as the vocal gifts. These are the gift of prophesy, the gift of tongues, and the gift of interpretation of tongues. As fascinating as these gifts are to observe in operation, God's love trumps all of them. That's why chapter 13 was written to these Corinthian believers. Many of them were flaunting their particular gift; they were boasting to one another about what gift they'd been given. It was pride on their part.

God's love needed to be involved in the operation of these gifts. That's what the first three verses of chapter 13 were trying to communicate. Paul sought to touch upon each of the nine gifts in those first three verses. In effect, he was telling them that even if they had all those gifts in operation, they could still use them with selfish orientation. If that was the case they would have no heavenly reward from the Lord whatsoever.

The gifts of the Spirit are for effective, powerful service for the Lord during our pilgrimage on earth. God desires that we draw upon these gifts to benefit our marriages, our families, and with all of our relationships. It's only after this is made clear to the Corinthian believers that Paul continues on in chapter 14. There Paul says in effect, "Now that we understand that there are gifts of the Spirit, now that we understand that God's love has to govern their use, here's what it looks like in action when the church gathers together. All the exercising of the gifts of the Spirit needed to be done decently and in order, with God's love overseeing their usage."

## NOW AND THEN

Let's take a look at 1 Corinthians 13:8-9:

**1 Corinthians 13:8-9**
*"⁸ Love never fails. But whether there are prophecies, they will fail; whether there are tongues, they will cease; whether there is knowledge, it will vanish away. ⁹ For we know in part and we prophesy in part."*

When Paul was speaking of knowledge here, he was not talking about the accumulation of facts and figures. I believe he was referring to the particular gift of the word of knowledge, because he'd been talking about the gifts of the Spirit in this section. So these verses refer to the word of knowledge, the gift of prophesy, and the gift of the speaking in other languages. Paul says, "Yes, these gifts are for now, but they're only temporary and they aren't going to last forever."

Paul, in this section, writes with a 'now and then' reasoning. Now we have this, but then face to face, and he goes from this life to the time when we'll meet the Lord face to face. Understand he's doing this because these Corinthians are so focused on their spiritual gifts that they had forgotten they were only for temporary use. Our hope is in what the Lord is going to do with us forever. Yes, these gifts are good for now, but we're not to make them the main focus of our life. Take a look at what God is going to be doing with us throughout eternity; keep that focus and we'll be more balanced.

Paul does refer to general knowledge in 1 Corinthians 8:1-3:

**1 Corinthians 8:1-3**
*"¹ Now concerning things offered to idols: We know that we all have knowledge. Knowledge puffs up, but love edifies. ² And if anyone thinks that he knows anything, he knows nothing yet as he ought to know. ³ But if anyone loves God, this one is known by Him."*

Our earthly knowledge is only partial compared to all things that exist, seen and unseen, in our universe. It's important to have a good understanding and reasoning to search out things. But we need to understand that in our learning, we're only scratching the surface of the mountain of what is there. The important thing to God is that we're controlled by Him, by His love, and that we love others with His love. That's what changes people.

Knowledge is not going to truly change people; God's love will change people. God's love will change us. Our spouse may be able to quote Scripture after Scripture regarding marriage, but are they living it out in love? Are they walking in love? I've seen far too many husbands use Scriptures to verbally and emotionally beat down their wives, and yet they aren't walking in God's love. It doesn't matter what we know. It matters how we live. Are we walking in God's love, or are we using the Bible as a cover for our own lack of love?

I've watched families that seem to have very strict discipline with their children. They're trying to be obedient to specific Scriptures found in the book of Proverbs, but they aren't listening to their children at all. They only hang onto those words, "Spare the rod, spoil the child" yet they don't see that their child is building a wall in their heart between them and their parent. Why? Because the parent isn't stopping to take into consideration the real issue. There's a breakdown in understanding what God's love looks like in their family. We may be a skilled Bible counselor to those who are needy, but are we letting God's love control our own life in every way?

Love trumps knowledge; it doesn't mean knowledge is unnecessary. It means that God's love needs to oversee the usage of that knowledge.

## WHEN THAT WHICH IS PERFECT HAS COME

### 1 Corinthians 13:9-10
*"⁹ For we know in part and we prophesy in part. ¹⁰ But when that which is perfect has come, then that which is in part will be done away."*

As we fellowship with other believers, we may come across those who've been taught that some of the gifts of the Spirit are no longer for today. They believe that certain gifts mentioned in this chapter were only for the first century for the establishing of the church. They were only to be used by the apostles. They believe that since the apostles have laid the biblical foundation of the church, we no longer need these gifts of the Spirit for our day. We have the full canon of Scripture to rely upon now. Our responsibility is to be obedient to what it says.

This is being taught in many seminaries and Bible colleges across the world today. All Christians believe that the baptism with the Holy Spirit is for every believer in every generation. But when it comes to the gifts of the Spirit, we're going to find fellow believers that can't go along with the operation of every gift of the Spirit for today.

Understand this: they love the Lord. They want to do what is right in the sight of the Lord. But sometimes I believe they are parroting what they've been told, rather than truly seeing it for themselves in the context with how it's simply stated in the New Testament.

Verse 10, *"But when that which is perfect has come"*, has been interpreted by many as referring to the Bible as a completed work. They believe the phrase 'that which is perfect' refers to the completed canon of Scripture. And since we now have the completed canon, certain gifts of the Spirit are no longer necessary for today. But here is my question. When you look at the context of this section, do you really think Paul was saying, "Boy, it's sure going to be nice when we finally get all the epistles written and collected"? I don't think that's what Paul had on his heart when we compare chapters 12, 13, and 14.

So what was Paul trying to drive home to them? I believe 'that which is perfect is come' has to do with that time when we, as a church, are brought before the Lord Jesus at His coming. At that time we'll see the fullness we were unable to see before. Right now, we know in part; right now, we prophecy in part; these are for this life until we get to that moment in time when we'll see Jesus face to face.

Then Paul uses verse 11 as an illustration of this: *"When I was a child I thought as a child, understood as a child, spoke as a child; but when I became a man, I put away childish things."*

In verse 12, the very first word is 'for,' which shows that it's connected to what had just been said, *"for now we see in a mirror, dimly."* We see reflections; we see parts of the reality. We don't know what heaven is like, but we can see little snapshots, little glimpses and flashes of things here and there as we read the Word. But we can't comprehend the fullness of what it's going to be like to experience the throne room of God. Just the very awe of the experience, the sound of the angels and the whole venue, we can't comprehend that here in this life.

We know in part, we prophecy in part, but when that which is perfect and mature and fulfilled has come, when we're brought before the Lord and changed into our glorified bodies, then we can more fully comprehend the reality of heaven.

## CAUGHT UP TO MEET THE LORD

There's coming a time, and I believe very soon, when all believers in Christ Jesus will be changed in a moment, in the twinkling of an eye. Here is what 1 Corinthians 15 says:

**1 Corinthians 15:50-54**
*"⁵⁰ Now this I say, brethren, that flesh and blood cannot inherit the kingdom of God; nor does corruption inherit incorruption. ⁵¹ Behold, I tell you a mystery: We shall not all sleep, but we shall all be changed— ⁵² in a moment, in the twinkling of an eye, at the last trumpet. For the trumpet will sound, and the dead will be raised incorruptible, and we shall be changed. ⁵³ For this corruptible must put on incorruption, and*

*this mortal must put on immortality.* [54] *So when this corruptible has put on incorruption, and this mortal has put on immortality, then shall be brought to pass the saying that is written: 'Death is swallowed up in victory.'* [50] *Now this I say, brethren, that flesh and blood cannot inherit the kingdom of God; nor does corruption inherit incorruption."*

In other words, we're going to need a glorified body to experience the reality of heaven when we meet the Lord.

The Greek word for mystery means 'a secret that was previously hidden, but is now revealed.' *We shall not all sleep,* referring to death; *but we shall all be changed*— referring to the change of our physical body into a glorified body. That's what happens at the event referred to in 1 Thessalonians 4:16-17, commonly referred to as the rapture of the church. And in the context of the previous verses of 1 Corinthians 15, this means that our physical body will be transformed into a glorified body in a millisecond, the twinkling of an eye. How fast does an eye twinkle? That's the reflection of light off your eyeball. The speed of light is approximately 186,000 miles per second. So, if we're counting on repenting at the very last second before that trumpet sounds, it's too late.

## FAITH, HOPE, AND LOVE

I believe the Bible is true. It's God's revelation of Himself, His revelation to us of what we're like, and of what's going to happen in the future. Right now, we live by faith, we live by hope, and we live by love, but faith and hope are for this life only. God's love goes on into eternity.

**Romans 8:24-25**

*"*[24] *For we were saved in this hope, but hope that is seen is not hope; for why does one still hope for what*

*he sees? ²⁵ But if we hope for what we do not see, we*
*eagerly wait for it with perseverance. "*

Hope is for this life, and then we're going to see Jesus
face to face. It's interesting to see the different Scriptures
that link faith and hope. Here are a few of them:

**1 Thessalonians 1:3-4**
*"³ remembering without ceasing your work of faith,*
*labor of love, and patience of hope in our Lord Jesus*
*Christ in the sight of our God and Father, ⁴ knowing*
*beloved brethren your election by God. "*

Work of faith means they put 'feet to their faith.' It wasn't
an empty dogma for them. It was something they believed
in, and it led to action in their life. The word labor means
'excessive toil, difficulty in carrying out the task.' What
motivated their sacrifice was God's love. Then we read of
their patience of hope; they had a hope of what lay on the
other side, a hope that was worth enduring all the hardship
they'd gone through and would continue to go through.

When we go through hardships in this life, it's important
that we fill our hearts with the reality of the hope that's
set before us. We must keep in mind the inheritance that's
going to be given to us when we meet the Lord. We could
lose everything here on earth, but we have this glorious
inheritance.

God is calling us to exercise faith in our marriages, to
take the situations that come up, as well as the conflicts and
the pressures, and ask God to help us apply faith in Him.

Let's exercise faith with our children. God doesn't tell
us His plan for our children. He doesn't give us the details,
but He does tell us how we're to surround them with His
nurture and admonition. Nurture means how we feed them,

how we give them an environment for healthy growth and perspective.

Admonition means that there are times when we're going to have to tell them no in love, just as the Lord does with us. But we do it in a loving way as He does with us. Yet the details of what they're going to do when they get older are the Lord's secret.

Even when our children go into a time of rebellion, God already knows what they're going to do, when and for how long. He has His boundaries concerning them. They think they're running from the Lord, but they don't realize they are on a kind of belt-line highway and they'll be coming right back around. The Lord brings them around for another confrontation, for another change.

We're to exercise hope in the Lord with our marriages, with our families, and with all our relationships. But above all, we're to exercise God's love in everything.

## CONCLUDING THOUGHTS

All sixteen of these attributes are natural expressions of God's love. Since love is the fruit of the Holy Spirit, what's needful in our lives is that we be filled to overflowing with His Spirit. God's love will change our lives. Our part is to join Him in His work within us, upon us, and through us. This life is too short to dally around and put this off for another day.

This work of God within us is not dependent upon our detailed knowledge of how it works. He's looking for us to simply believe Him, yield to Him, and invite Him to have full rights over our lives. There's nothing to fear in Him. Absolute surrender is absolute adventure and blessing. May we open our hearts to Him ready for the adventure.

# DISCUSSION GUIDE

The following questions are to help facilitate discussion within small group settings. After each person has read the chapter, there'll be five questions based on that chapter. These are designed to stimulate further considerations.

There are five basic guidelines which are very important to agree upon within every small group:

1.) Confidentiality: what is shared within the group stays within the group.

2.) No interrupting: when someone is opening up and sharing something about their life or their opinion on a subject, let them finish out their thoughts.

3.) No advice giving: the small group setting is not the time for counseling; that can occur one on one after the group is finished.

4.) No probing: sometimes when a person opens up about their life, it's the first time they've ever let that wall down; let them share to the level of their own comfort.

5.) No judging: when a person has opened themselves to the group and shared a deep problem in their own lives, it's not the time for quick judgments and rebukes; just listen and pray for one another.

The questions on each chapter may also be used in personal devotional times to draw you closer in your relationship with Christ.

For those of you who are in a small group setting, please take the time to pray for one another after the time of discussion. If you're using these questions in your personal devotions, lift up these answers to the Lord and ask Him to fill you with His love.

## Chapter 1: Our True Soulmate

1. In our younger years, we probably picked up some expectations of what it was going to feel like when we found our true soulmate. What were some of your expectations?

2. When our dreams of finding that perfect soulmate have been shattered, many are reluctant to enter new relationships right away. What are some of the reasons people withdraw after a broken relationship?

3. Since God created us He knows that we need to love and be loved. He's designed us to be filled with His love as a foundation. Have you ever come to the place in your life where you've embraced His love as the foundation for true love? If so, when did that happen and what was it like for you?

4. God's love for us is not based on our inherent goodness or our good deeds. It's unconditional. Yet many times we slip into a 'performance mode' when we think about being accepted by Him. What have been some ways in the past that you have defaulted to a performance mode as you have related to God?

5. Sometimes we withhold our love for others because they've not performed toward us in a way that we found acceptable. But as Christians, we're commanded to love them with God's love, not our own love. What makes it difficult for us to let go of that performance-based love when it comes to other people? Our spouse (if married)? Our children (if applicable)? Our coworkers?

## CHAPTER 2: SATURATED WITH HIS LOVE

1. As we journey through life, we encounter people that are very difficult to love. Yet God has called us to be saturated with His love and to let the overflow splash down on others. What are some of the reasons it is difficult to love those people?

2. This chapter touched upon the subject of coming to the place in our lives where we only want what God wants for us. What are some of the things that cause us to hold back from that kind of desire?

3. Sometimes people can become consumed in thoughts of their worthlessness, uselessness, and self-loathing. But God's love can set them free from those destructive mindsets. What are some ways we can let God's love flow out from us to them to help them let go and be healed of those mindsets?

4. As believers in Christ Jesus, we've been given the Spirit of God as a gift and a down payment of our eternal inheritance. God's Spirit communes with our spirit about how very much He loves us. If we could place our spirit within another person we love so dearly, what would we want them to know and feel?

5. Mention was made in this chapter about how golf balls displace water in a pitcher. But when those golf balls are removed, more water can be poured into that pitcher. Imagine your life like that pitcher and the water being God's Spirit. What areas of your life could be a 'golf ball' that keeps you from a deeper experience of God's love?

## CHAPTER 3: LOVE IS PATIENT

1. Longsuffering is an attribute of God. This is reinforced time and again throughout Scripture. Yet many people view God as hasty in His judgments and harsh in His treatment of those who aren't living in total holiness. Why do you think some people come to this kind of idea about what God is like?

2. The word patient or longsuffering includes the idea of bearing ill treatment from others and continuing to care for them. Why do you think it's important not to close off your heart to someone who has offended you or hurt you in some way?

3. Impatience shows itself in many ways in our lives. What are some of the more common behaviors that have their origin in impatience?

4. All of us have been impatient at times. If not dealt with quickly it can soon produce destructive ends. Has there been a time in your life when impatience has cost you?

5. Responding to others with God's love will cause us to be more patient with people. It'll also change our perspective from quick judgments of others to compassion and mercy. Share a time when you noticed that God's love showed itself in patience toward others.

## CHAPTER 4: LOVE IS KIND

1. It was stated in this chapter that longsuffering and patience are love's inner strength, while kindness is one of the first outward expressions of God's love. Can you think of an instance where a Christian showed you exceptional kindness?

2. The Scriptures have much to say about God's lovingkindness. How has God's lovingkindness impacted your life over the years?

3. Many times people will start out being kind toward others, but end up becoming so critical, harsh, and unkind. What may have happened along the way to cause this to occur?

4. Being filled with God's love will show itself in kindness toward others. Yet even Christians can become so unkind in their actions toward other Christians. Why do you think kindness is too vulnerable for some people to express?

5. There may have been times in our recent past when we've been quite unkind to someone. Maybe they caught us off-guard or we were exceptionally tired. Are there people that you need to approach and ask their forgiveness for your unkind attitude, words, or actions?

## CHAPTER 5: LOVE DOES NOT ENVY

1. The chapter stated that God's love has no selfish envy in any way. The goal of His love is to enrich the object of that love and to rejoice when blessings are poured out upon another. Yet most of us have struggled at times with feelings of envy over another's windfall. Why do we sometimes think it unfair when others are blessed?

2. Contentment and satisfaction are antonyms of envy. When God's love is filling our lives contentment and a thankful heart will be the byproduct. Describe a time when God worked in your life to bring about a thankful heart.

3. When envy is taking hold in our hearts, it will show itself in certain attitudes, words, or actions. What comes to your mind when you think of a person expressing their envy?

4. We all have experienced envy at one point or another in our lives. Share an instance when envy seemed to get a strong foothold in your interactions with others.

5. Envy drains us of energy, saps us of life, and eats us up from the inside out. God's love invigorates, is life-giving, and restores our soul. In what area of your life do you need God to touch you and wash you with His love?

## CHAPTER 6: LOVE IS NOT SELF-CENTERED

1. When we think of someone parading around and boasting of their accomplishments there may be a person that comes to our minds. Without mentioning their name, what is it about that person that shows itself in self-centeredness?

2. 'Puffed up' is a description of an inward attitude of self-importance. It has its basis in sinful pride. But striving for excellence is different than having an inflated view of self-importance. What do you think would be the line that's crossed for a person to go from striving for excellence to ending up having an inflated view of self-importance?

3. Some people have grown up in homes where the atmosphere of rudeness was the norm. It now has become second nature to them. When someone is rude to you, what does it feel like? Why is it a challenge to love them back?

4. Rudeness can also be covered with crafty rationalizations. For instance, when saving money is the bottom line we can think that it doesn't matter how we get to that goal. Can you remember a time when someone was rude to you just to get you to lower your standards?

5. God's love is not self-centered. When His love saturates our hearts we become others' oriented rather than self-oriented. We'll treat others with respect and honor. Is there a situation right now where you know it's time for you to choose to honor another person?

## CHAPTER 7: LOVE DOES NOT HAVE A SHORT FUSE

1.  Looking back on your home life, would you say that the atmosphere of the home was one of peace and tranquility, or anger and chaos?

2.  All of us have had angry moments in our lives. Then after a while we cool off and look back on our explosion and see that it wasn't that big of a deal. Think of the last time you were angry. What was the cause of that anger?

3.  Control issues are a large part of what causes anger. We want to control our world outwardly because we feel so out of control inwardly. When someone or something comes along to disrupt that control, we explode in sinful anger. Are there any areas of your life that you feel are out of control right now?

4.  When God's love is flowing through our lives, anger won't be our master. The Holy Spirit will be right there to snuff out that sprout of anger when it rises up. Yet we must invite Him to help us. Can you recall a time in your Christian experience when you witnessed God's help in snuffing out an angry moment?

5.  Bitterness and unforgiveness are merciless masters. Although the offenses against us may be real and unjust, the soul damage is active and growing if left alone. Why is it so difficult to forgive someone who has deeply hurt us?

## CHAPTER 8: LOVE KEEPS NO RECORD OF WRONGS SUFFERED

1. God's love doesn't keep a record of wrongs suffered. This is the reality of our standing before Him in Christ. Yet when people sin against us, we can tend to mull over those offenses again and again, sometimes years later. What makes it feel so vulnerable for us to think of shredding their record of wrongs against us?

2. When we keep bringing up past offenses to someone who has hurt us, it usually doesn't bring about restoration of the relationship. For many people this is what caused their family to disintegrate. Are there relatives of yours who just can't let go of some past offenses?

3. When we place faith in Christ for our salvation, we're forgiven of all our sins, past, present, and future. Yet we still sin against God and others. That's when we can begin to think that God is keeping a record of wrongs suffered. What makes it so hard for us to receive the truth of God's forgiveness after we've sinned against Him?

4. God's love can heal a person's soul of all those wrongs they've suffered. But there must be an initial step of faith to release the offender to God and let go of the right to hurt back. If there's someone like this in your life right now, take that step of faith and release them to God.

5. There's tremendous freedom in forgiveness. Your entire outlook on life changes. It'll open the floodgates of God's love to flow through your life like never before. Ask the Lord to fill you with His love and heal the wounds deep within.

## CHAPTER 9: LOVE REJOICES IN THE TRUTH

1.  We used to rejoice in iniquity before we surrendered our lives to Christ. Now, as believers, we're to put away those thoughts and habits. Yet not all Christians do this. Have you ever met someone who said they were a Christian only to discover later how they delighted in scenarios of iniquity? How did that make you feel?

2.  The definition of sin is simply to 'miss the mark.' Even when we're trying to do what is right we can end up missing the mark by failing to obey God's word. Share a time when you were trying to do the right thing but it ended up worse than when you started.

3.  God's love doesn't rejoice when another person's life falls apart because of their sin. Rather, there's true grief over what has taken place. Have you ever had someone be actually glad that things went from bad to worse in your life?

4.  Many times you'll hear the statement, "All truth is God's truth." Since truth is defined as 'that which is conformable to fact,' it's imperative that the facts are solid. Have you ever believed something was true in the past that you now know was not true at all?

5.  The Bible tells us the truth about God, ourselves, and our world. Yet popular opinion can so contradict the Bible. What opinions of others have you encountered that have gone against the Word of God?

## CHAPTER 10: LOVE BEARS, BELIEVES, HOPES, ENDURES ALL THINGS

1. Because of our love for another person we may have had to make great personal sacrifices. Share a time when this has been true in your life.

2. God's love believes all things. This includes the idea of believing the best first. Yet we don't always walk in God's love when it comes to sizing up other people. Share a time when you made a rash judgment about another person only to find out later that you were completely wrong.

3. It's easy to believe the worst first about another person. The pressure to go along with the crowd in their rumors and gossip is very great. What makes it difficult to hold the line of God's love in these kinds of situations?

4. Sometimes we're so convinced that our circumstances are always directly related to God's approval or disapproval. This causes us to waver in our faith about God's promises. There are times, though, that we press through difficulties, hold onto God's promises, and He comes through with the blessing. Was there a time recently when this was the case?

5. God's love endures all things. He's able to give us that strength to make it through as we focus on Him. Most of us have had to endure difficulties in our lives. Share a time when the Lord gave you the courage and endurance to pull through a difficult time.

## CHAPTER 11: LOVE NEVER FAILS

1. God tells us over and over in Scripture that He loves us. This is for our sake because we need the affirmation. We love to hear it, but often we don't take the time to express our love to Him. Take a few moments to tell God how much you love Him.

2. God's love is constant, no matter what happens to us circumstantially. His love in us will cause us to love others unconditionally. Share a time when the reality of God's unconditional, constant love impacted your day.

3. We've all had times when everything around us came crashing down. It ended in so many broken pieces of our life. Yet God loves to take those pieces and make a beautiful mosaic out of them. How have you seen God begin this work of art with your broken pieces?

4. Loving someone with God's love includes times where correction and rebuke are necessary. The goal is always restoration with God and with others that have been offended. Yet many times Christians are reluctant to confront a fellow believer who's practicing sin. What makes it difficult to step into this aspect of God's love?

5. Sometimes in our life situation we can come to the end of ourselves and find that we're empty of God's love. That's the time to open our heart to Him and ask to be filled again. When was the last time you came to this point in your life?

## CHAPTER 12: THE GREATEST OF THESE IS LOVE

1. Often, when people feel they are losing their grip on life, they turn to destructive behaviors. Rather than helping their situation, they complicate things exponentially. But God still loves them unconditionally. Is there someone you know whose life is spinning out of control (don't give their name)? Take some time to pray for them right now.

2. Being in the eye of a hurricane is an illustration of what it's like abiding in the peace of God while all else around us was in chaos. Think back on your life. Was there a time when you experienced this supernatural peace of God?

3. Faith, hope, and love are foundation stones for our life here on earth as believers. When we meet the Lord Jesus face to face we'll no longer need faith or hope. But love will remain forever. What have been some of your thoughts about heaven? Can you remember any specific Scriptures that speak about heaven?

4. God has given to every believer at least one gift of the Spirit. These gifts are given to build up the body of Christ and to be used in our service to the Lord. After considering what was mentioned in this chapter, what gift or gifts of the Spirit have you seen operating through your life?

5. Our true inheritance is waiting for us in heaven. This will be far richer than any monies, positions, or possessions we could ever acquire while down here on earth. Why is it that we focus so much on earthly inheritance and so little on what awaits us in heaven?

# ABOUT THE AUTHOR

Bob Claycamp was born in Oregon into the Christian home of Elmer and Alta Claycamp. He and his older sister, Bev, were raised to believe that God existed and loved each person, and that Jesus was the Christ, the Son of God. But as Bob entered his teen years he began to wander from these biblical values established at home, and progressively entered the world of rock bands, drugs, and immorality. His parents prayed; Bob strayed.

When Bob was a sophomore in high school, his mother died of cancer. This further drove him to find the true meaning of life. He opened his mind to the occult and the paranormal, and his drug use increased.

A few times he almost killed himself in his quest to find answers. But after graduating from high school, he met some young people who were very zealous for Christ.

Since they were renting rooms in the big three story house the rock band had leased, this put the gospel of Jesus Christ right in his face day and night. After weeks of debate and discussion, the Holy Spirit began to draw him into a saving relationship with Jesus. He and his high school sweetheart, Jeanne, prayed to receive Christ as their Savior. Things in their life started changing immediately.

An elderly white-haired saddle maker named Nick Gray introduced himself to Bob and Jeanne on Sunday night at church and began to disciple them in the Scriptures. He told them about a youth ministry that had recently moved up to Eugene, Oregon from a church in California (Calvary Chapel of Costa Mesa), and took them to meet this group. From this point on, this youth ministry (Shiloh Youth Revival Centers) became the greenhouse for Bob and Jeanne's Christian growth and ministry experience.

Bob and Jeanne married at age eighteen in the beginning of 1970 and lived in several of the dormitory-style Christian youth houses that were springing up all over the United States. This was the beginning of an eight and a half year involvement with Shiloh. In 1973, they moved out to the main Study Center in Dexter, Oregon where Bob became one of the five teachers of the foundational Bible School for the youth ministry.

In 1978, Bob and Jeanne and their two sons, Micah and Jesse, moved to Arizona. After about three years selling insurance, and a third child later (Christopher), Bob began to pastor a small group of believers (1981) in the north part of Phoenix, which became known as Calvary Chapel-North Phoenix. Since this church began, it has planted and sent out many churches and ministries. Truly this has been the result of the grace of God working in their midst.

Bob and Jeanne have now entered a new aspect of their ministry: coming alongside other younger pastors and their wives to encourage them and offer assistance in any way that may be needed. They have joined the Poimen Ministries, a group of seasoned pastors, each with thirty or more years of ministry experience, that have this as their vision.

You can contact Pastor Bob and Jeanne Claycamp at these websites:

http://www.bobclaycamp.com
http://www.poimenministries.com
http://www.calvarynorth.com

# NOTES

# NOTES

# NOTES

# NOTES

# NOTES

# NOTES

# NOTES

# NOTES

# NOTES

# NOTES

# NOTES

# NOTES

# NOTES

_____

_____

_____

_____

_____

_____

_____

_____

_____

_____

_____

_____

_____

_____